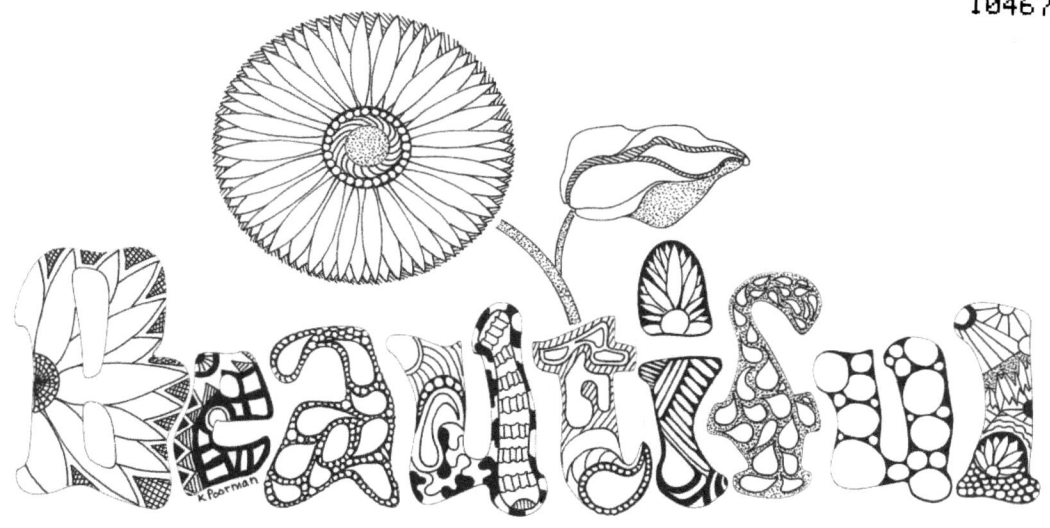

26 Beautiful Words to Color

by Kevin Poorman

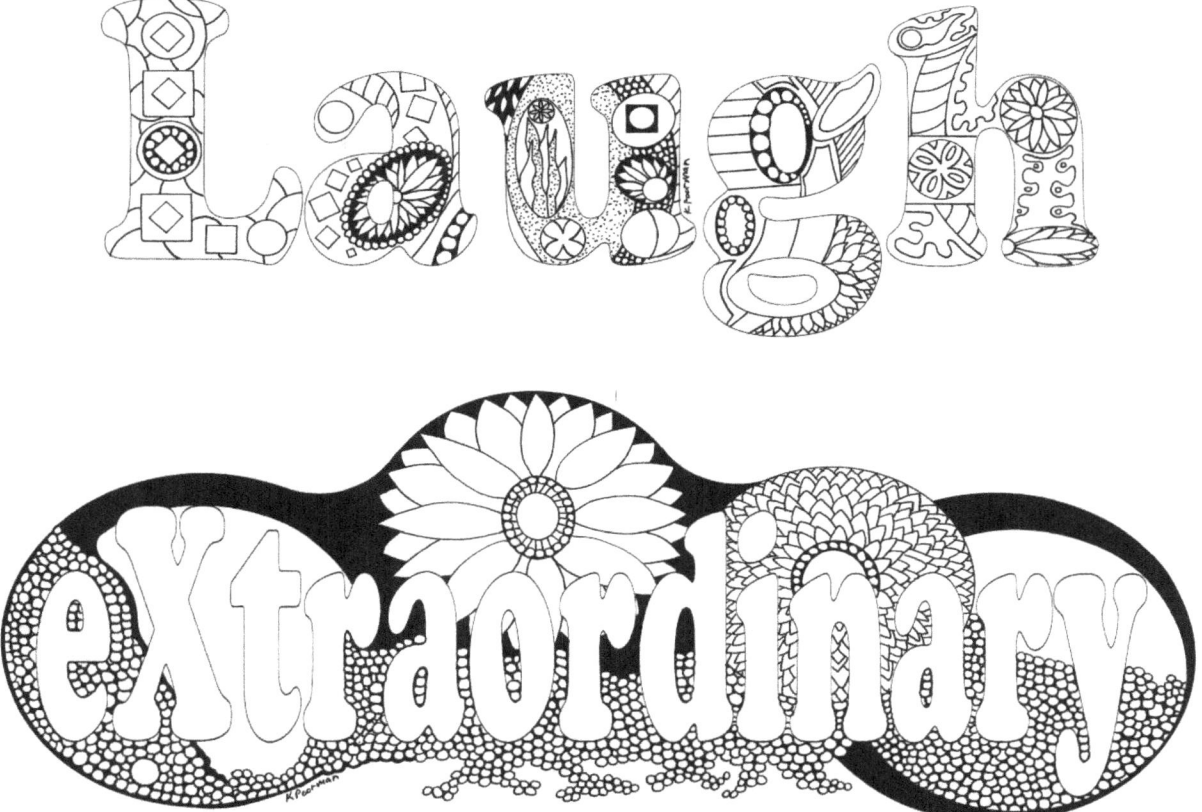

Poorman Doodles

Book 4

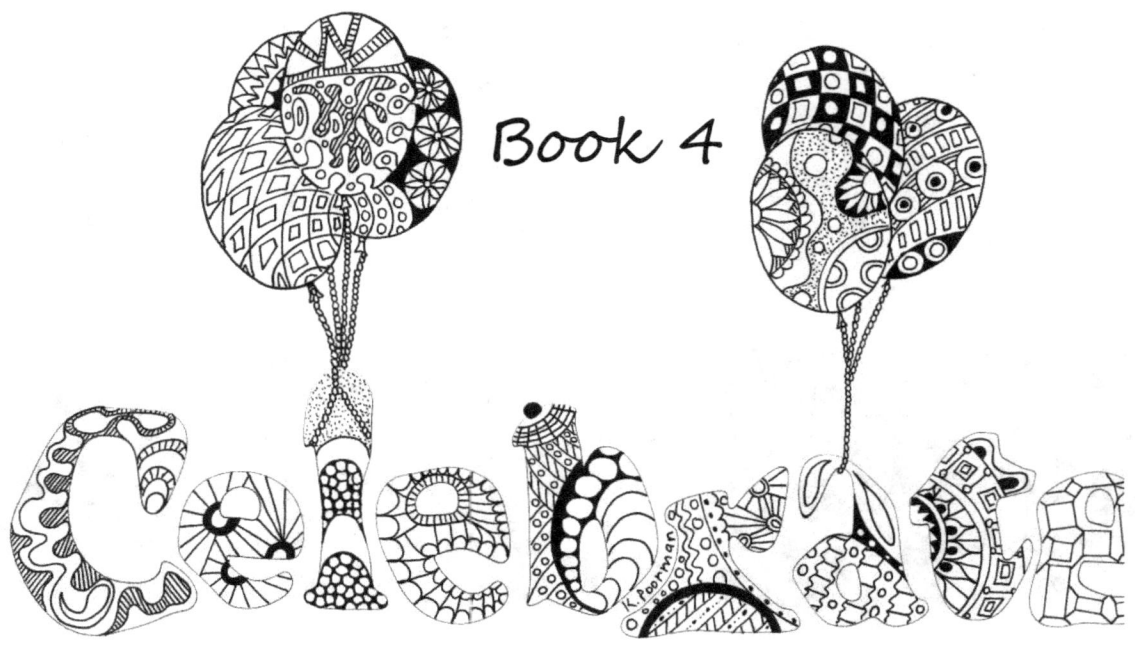

Celebrate

Beautiful Words

A to Z

About the Artist

Kevin Poorman is an artist, photographer and puzzle-maker living in Lorton, Virginia. He grew up in Southern Indiana where his family owned and operated an artist supplies and picture framing business catering to area artists and art students attending Vincennes University.

Kevin's preferred art medium is pen and black ink. This book contains doodles of 26 positive words from A to Z. Enjoy many hours coloring and reflecting on these words.

In the last few years, Kevin ventured into making jigsaw puzzles from his artwork and photographs. His puzzles are available at several historical venues in Northern Virginia, including George Mason's plantation at Gunston Hall, the Manassas National Battlefield, the Fairfax City Museum, as well as various gift and specialty shops, including Puzzle Palooza, Etc., in Occoquan, T & K Treasures Specialty Gifts in Clifton, and The Made in Virginia Store, Fredericksburg, Virginia.

Please see the full line of Kevin's drawings, photographs and puzzles at www.puzzlecuts.com .

Email comments to: puzzlecuts@gmail.com

Enjoy coloring in Book #4!

Contents

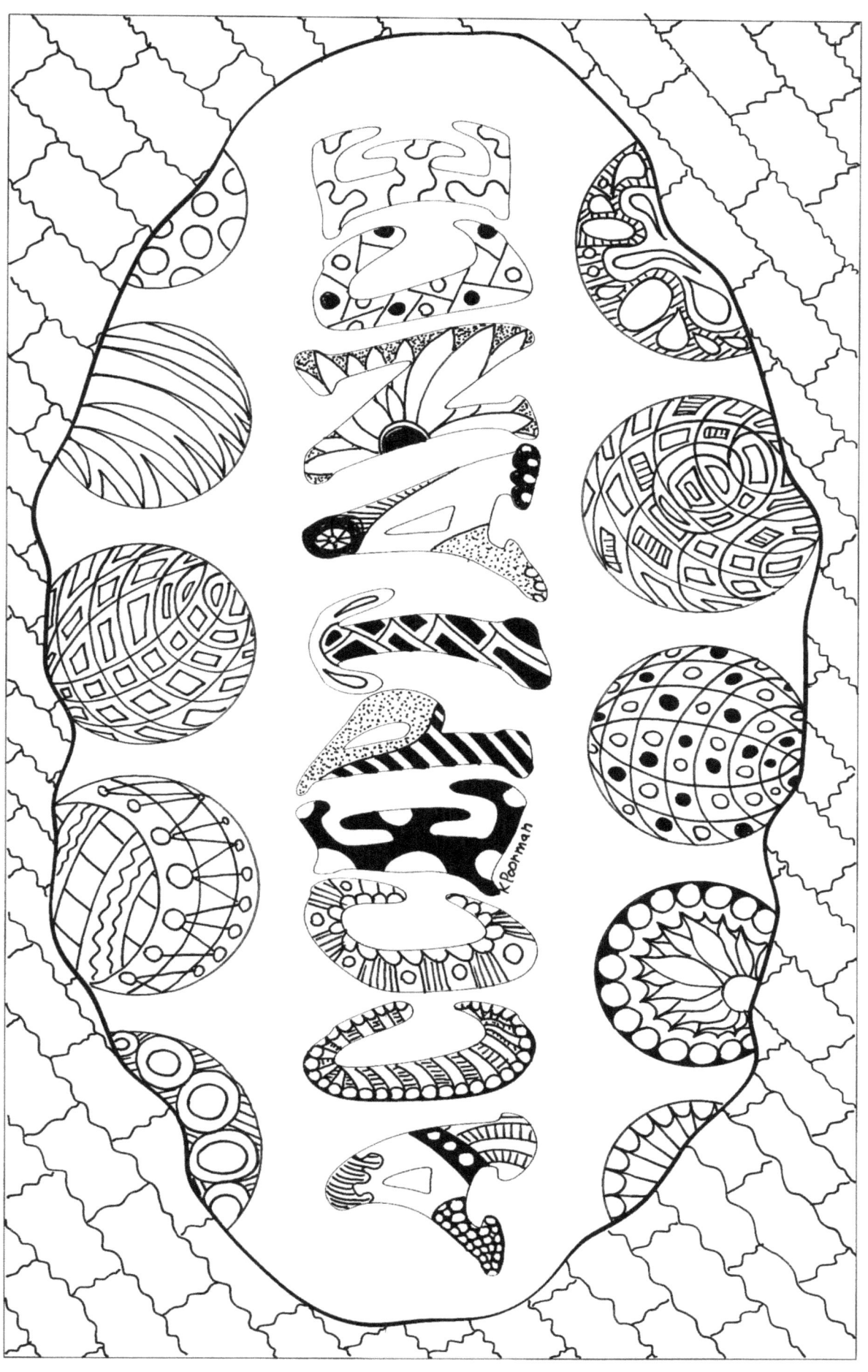

This blank page serves as a blotter page to absorb marker ink that might bleed through while coloring.

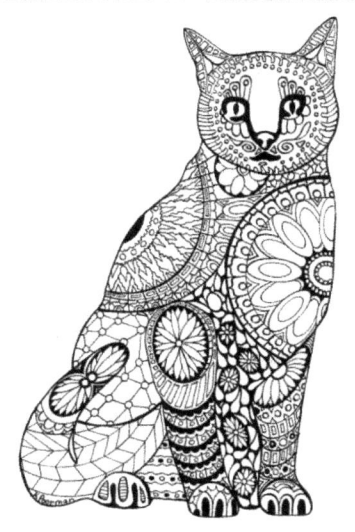

"The Cat" is in *Poorman Doodles*, Book 5

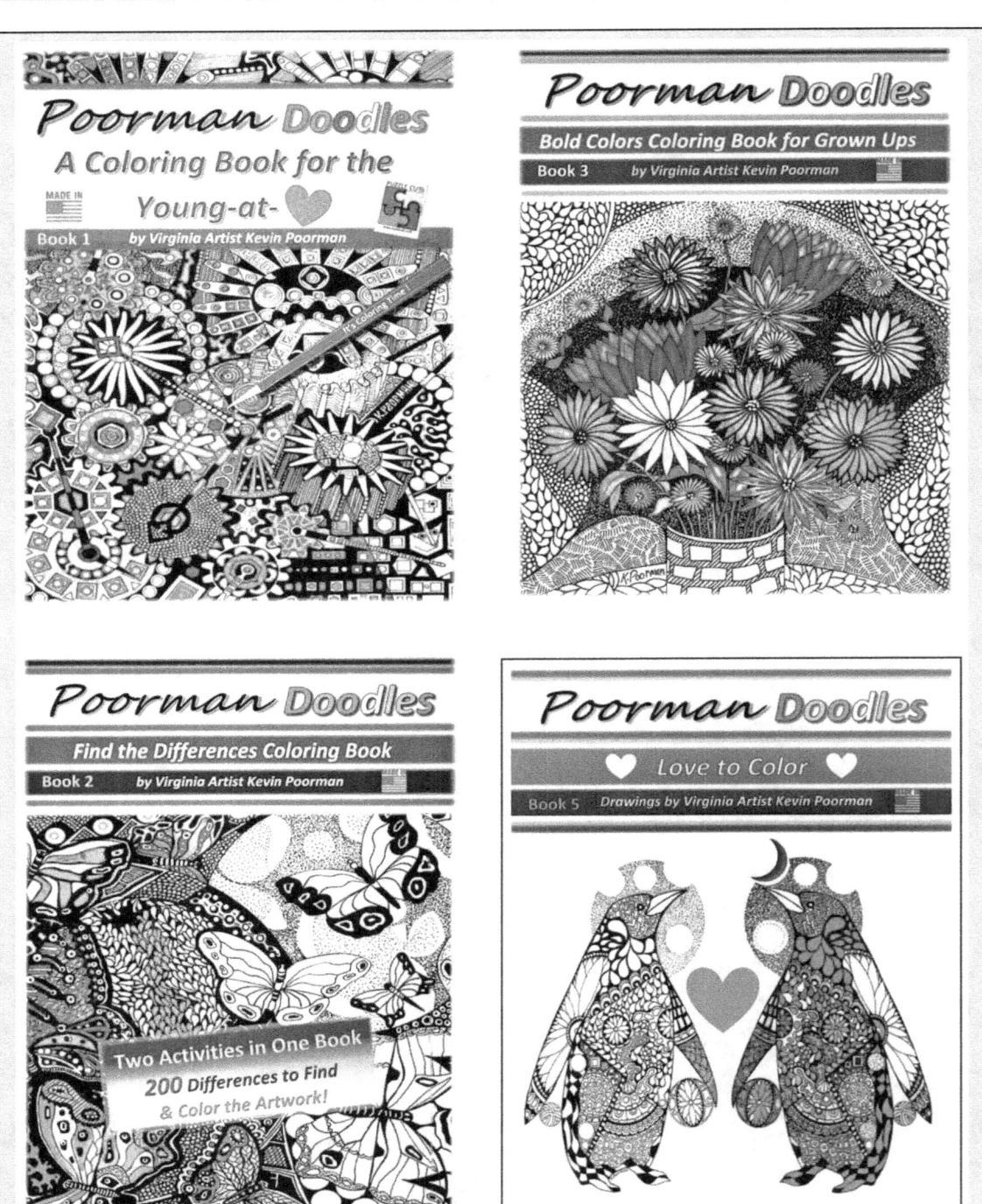

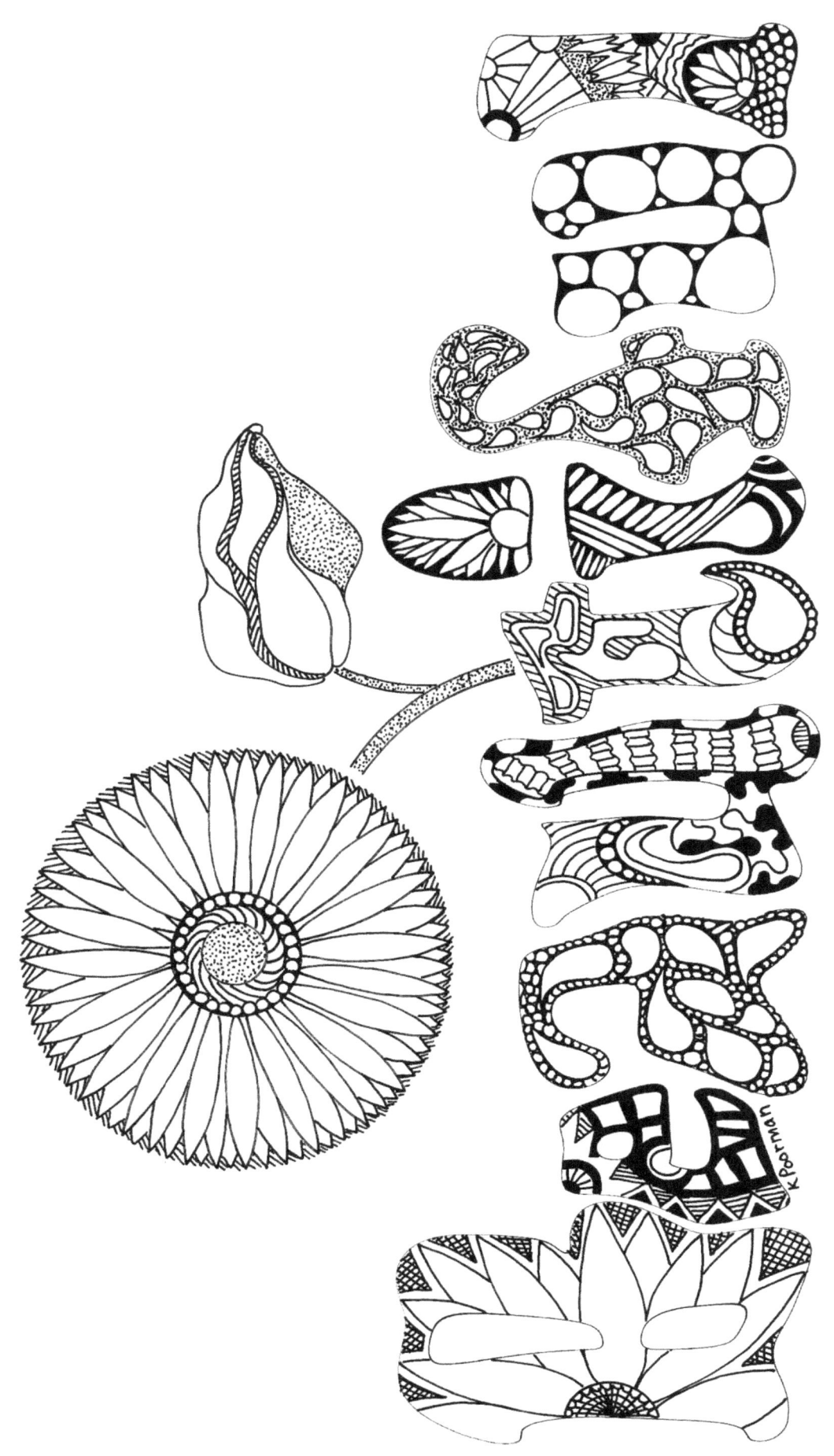

This blank page serves as a blotter page to absorb marker ink that might bleed through while coloring.

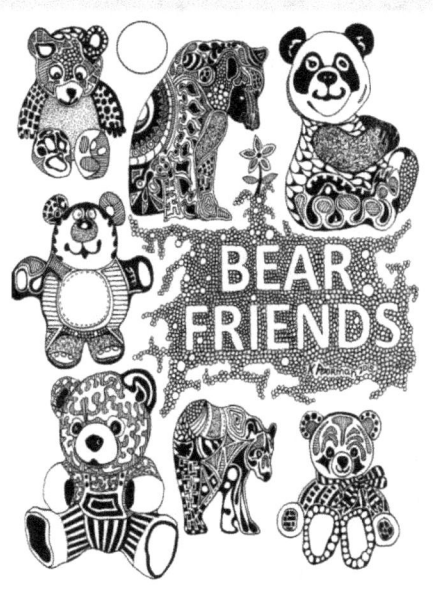

In *Poorman Doodles* book # 1

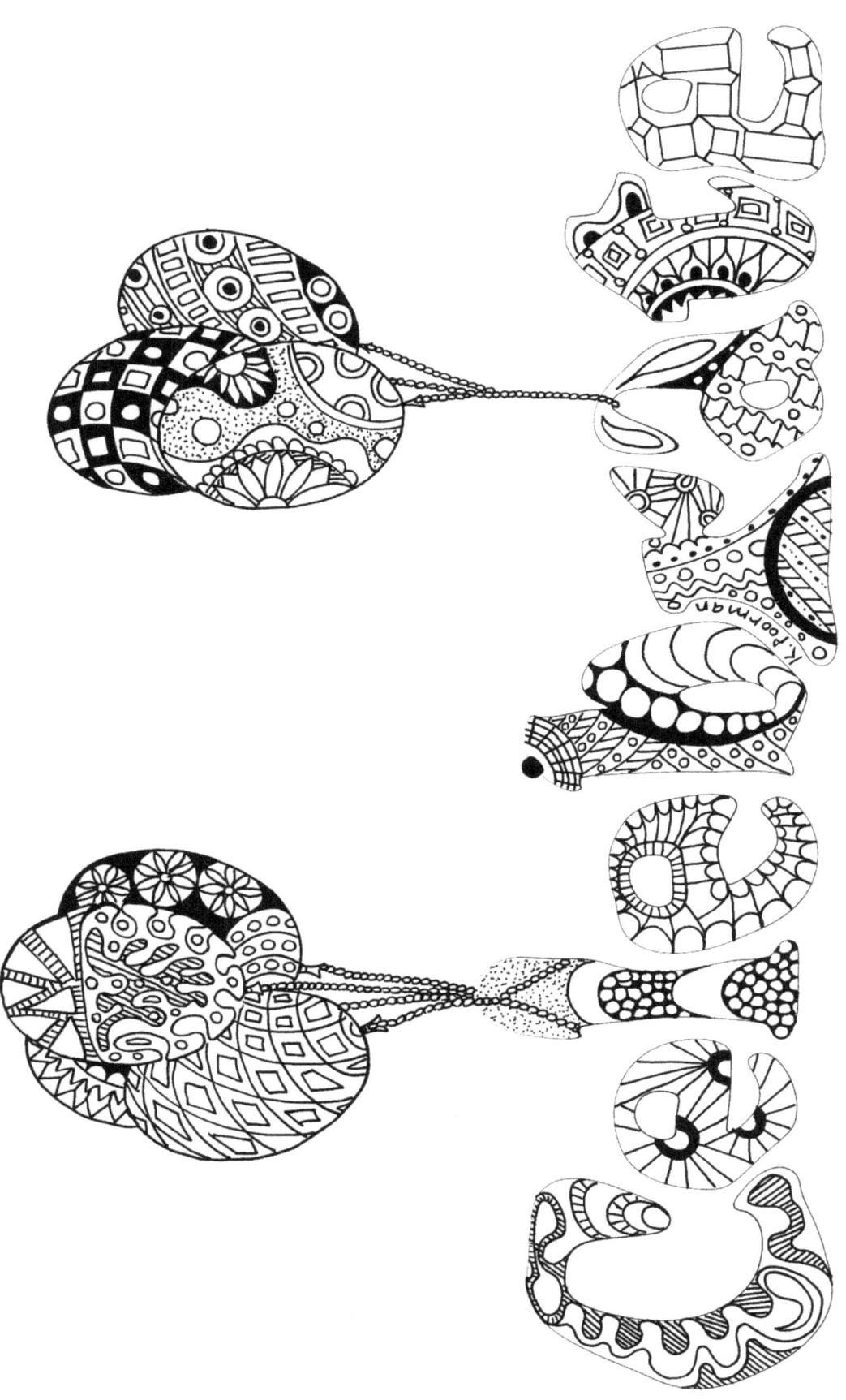

This blank page serves as a blotter page to absorb marker ink that might bleed through while coloring.

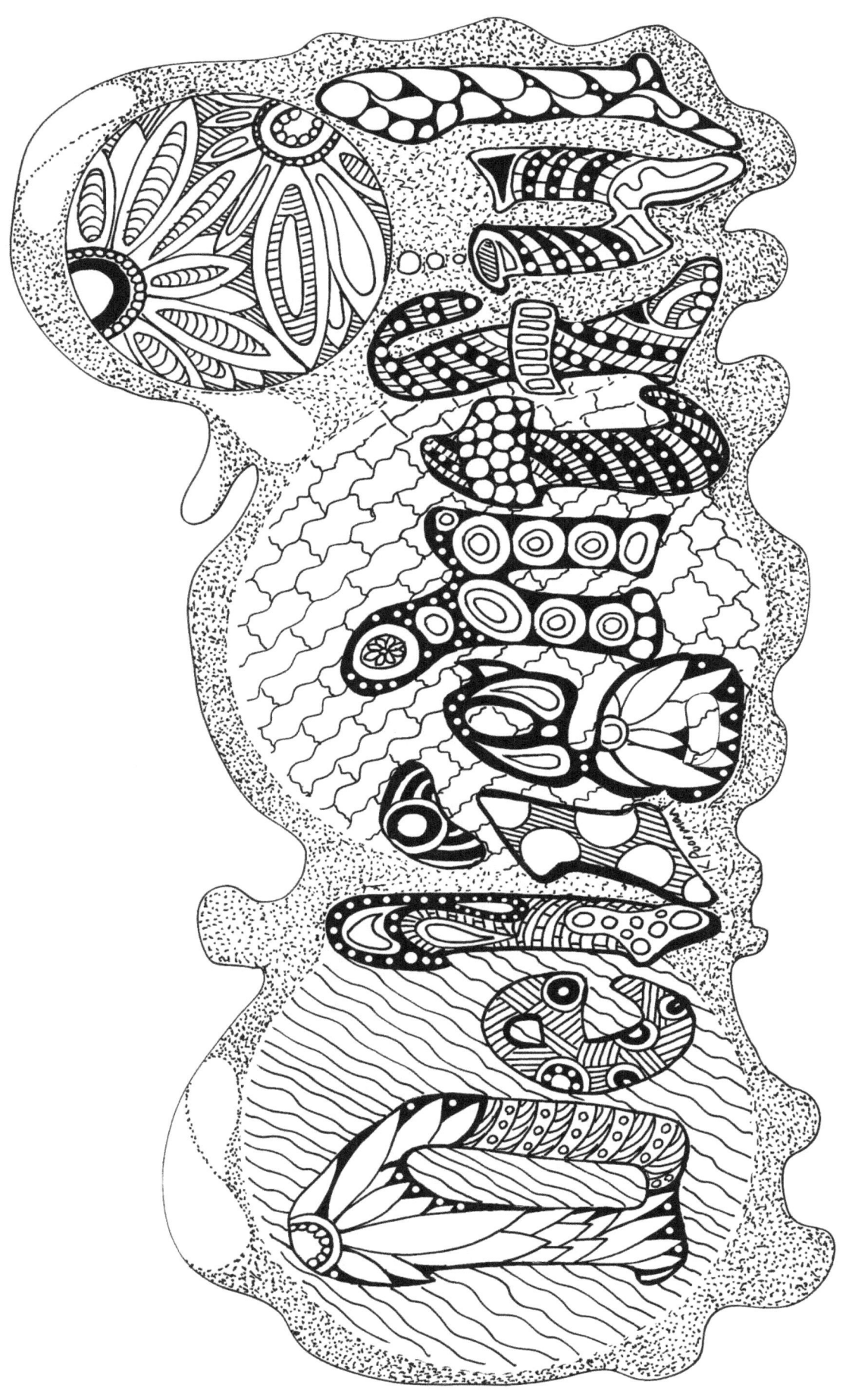

This blank page serves as a blotter
page to absorb marker ink that
might bleed through while coloring.

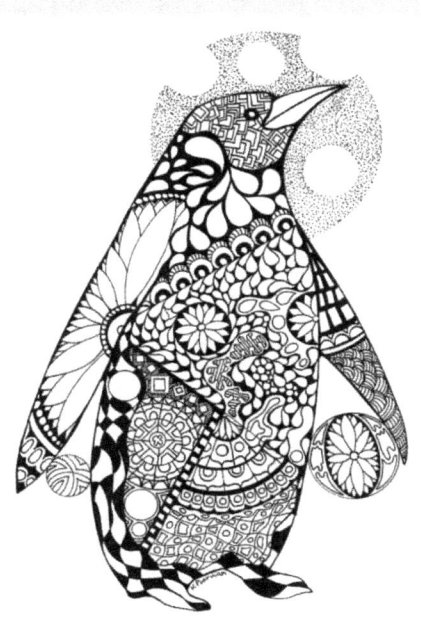

"The Penguin" is in *Poorman Doodles*, Book 5

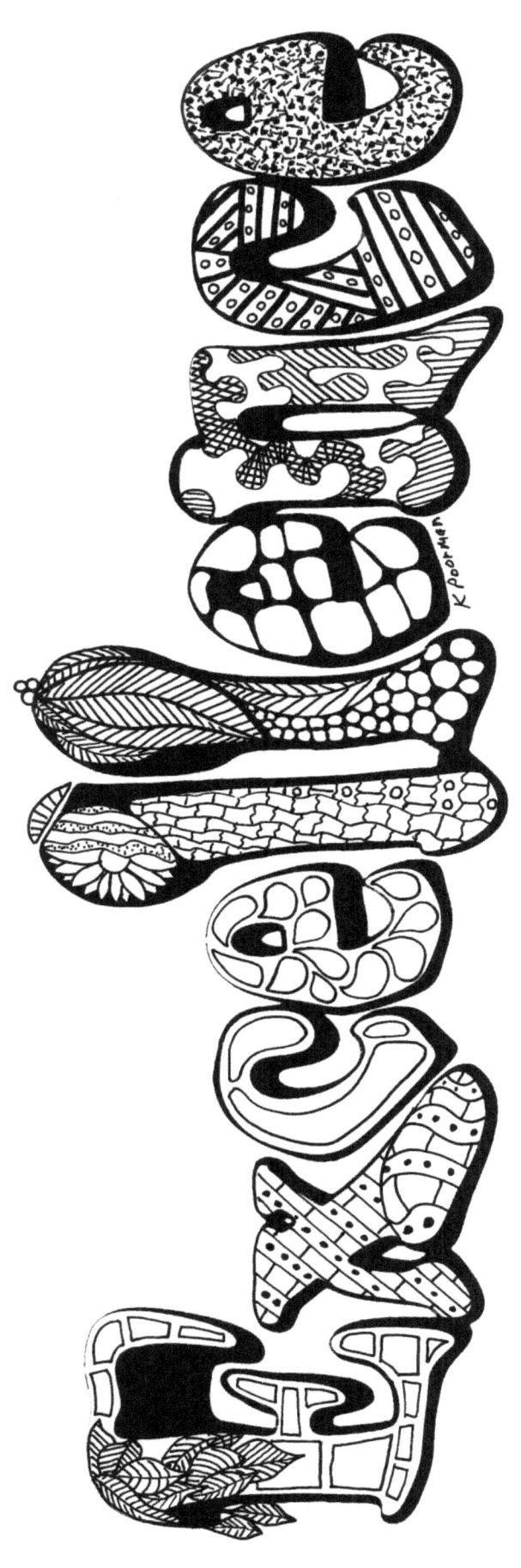

This blank page serves as a blotter page to absorb marker ink that might bleed through while coloring.

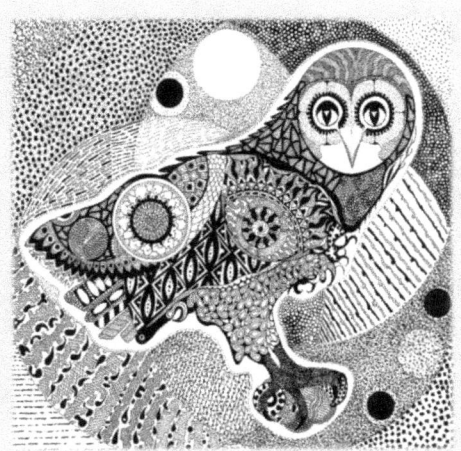

In Poorman Doodles book # 1.

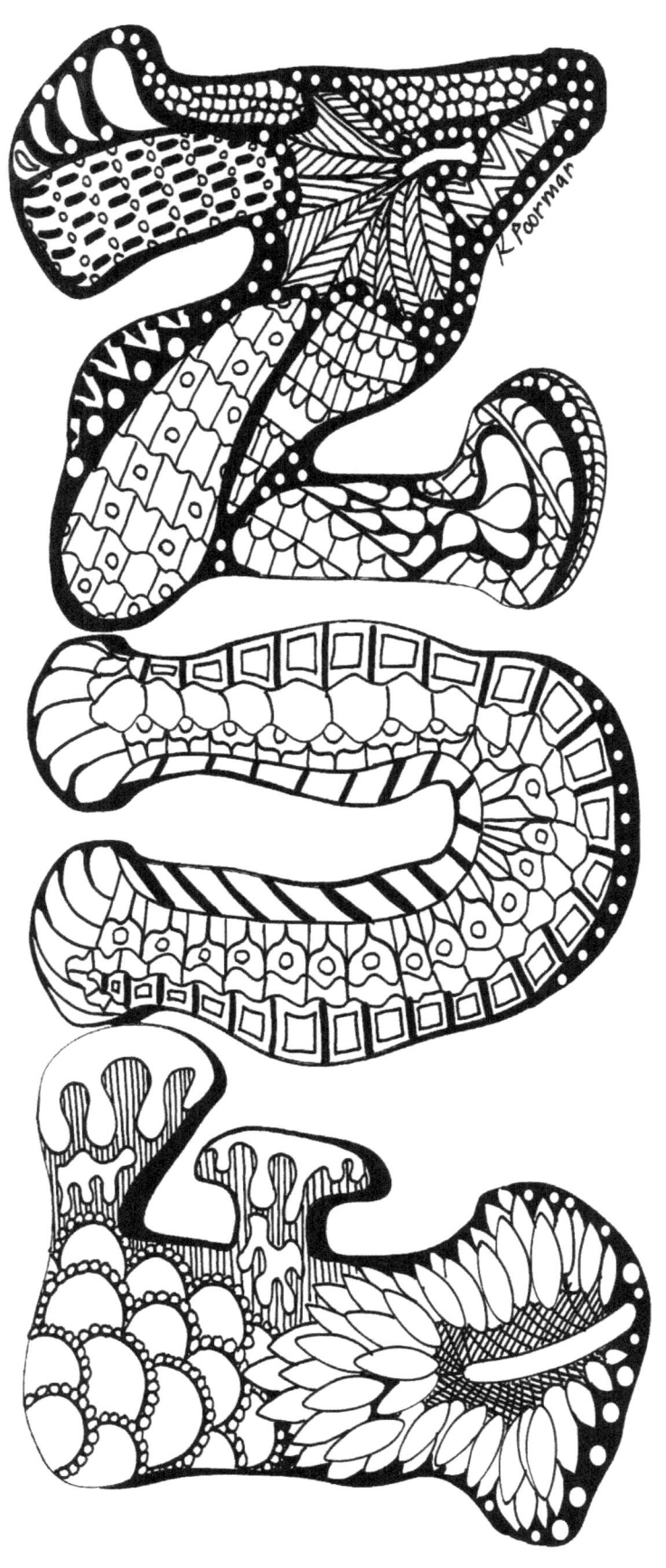

This blank page serves as a blotter
page to absorb marker ink that
might bleed through while coloring.

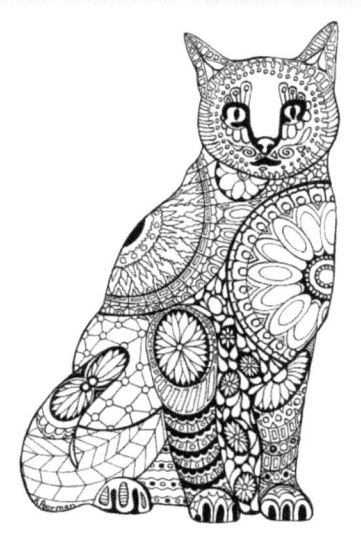

"The Cat" is in *Poorman Doodles*, Book 5

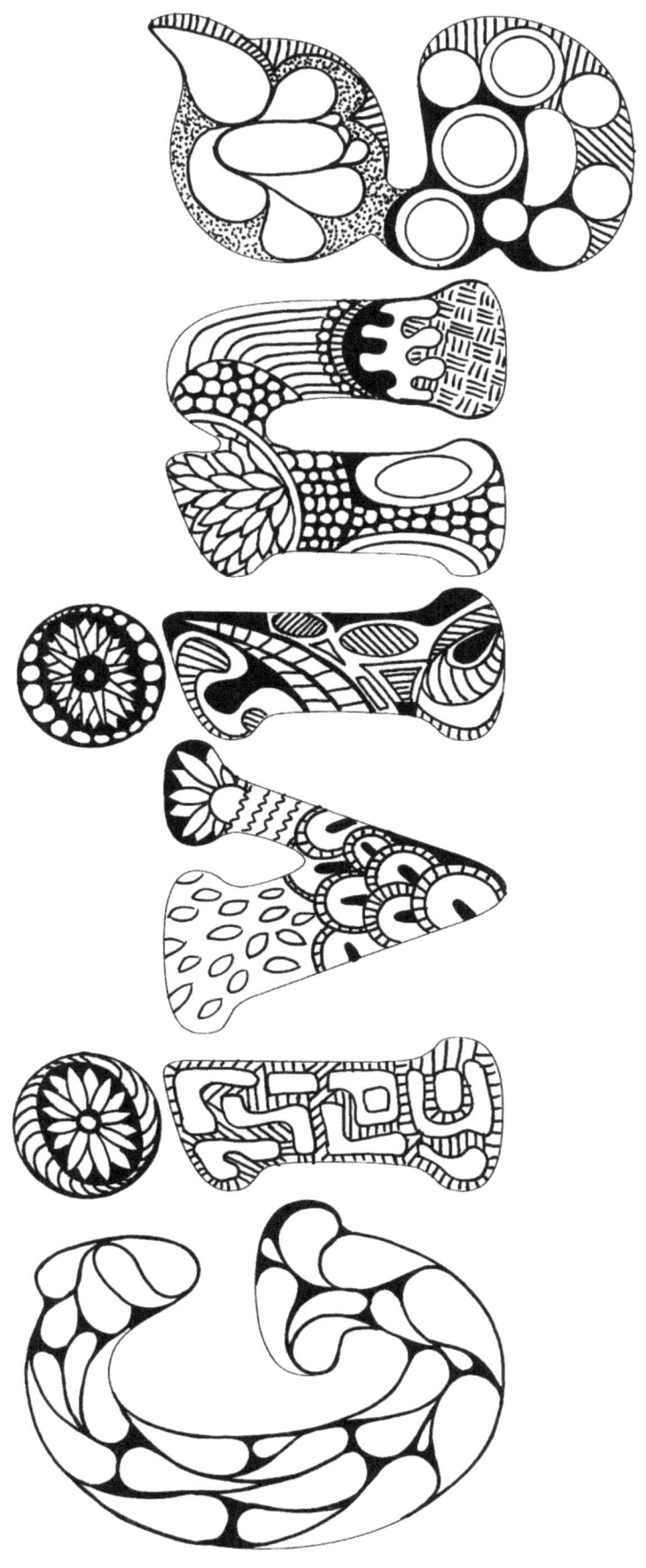

This blank page serves as a blotter page to absorb marker ink that might bleed through while coloring.

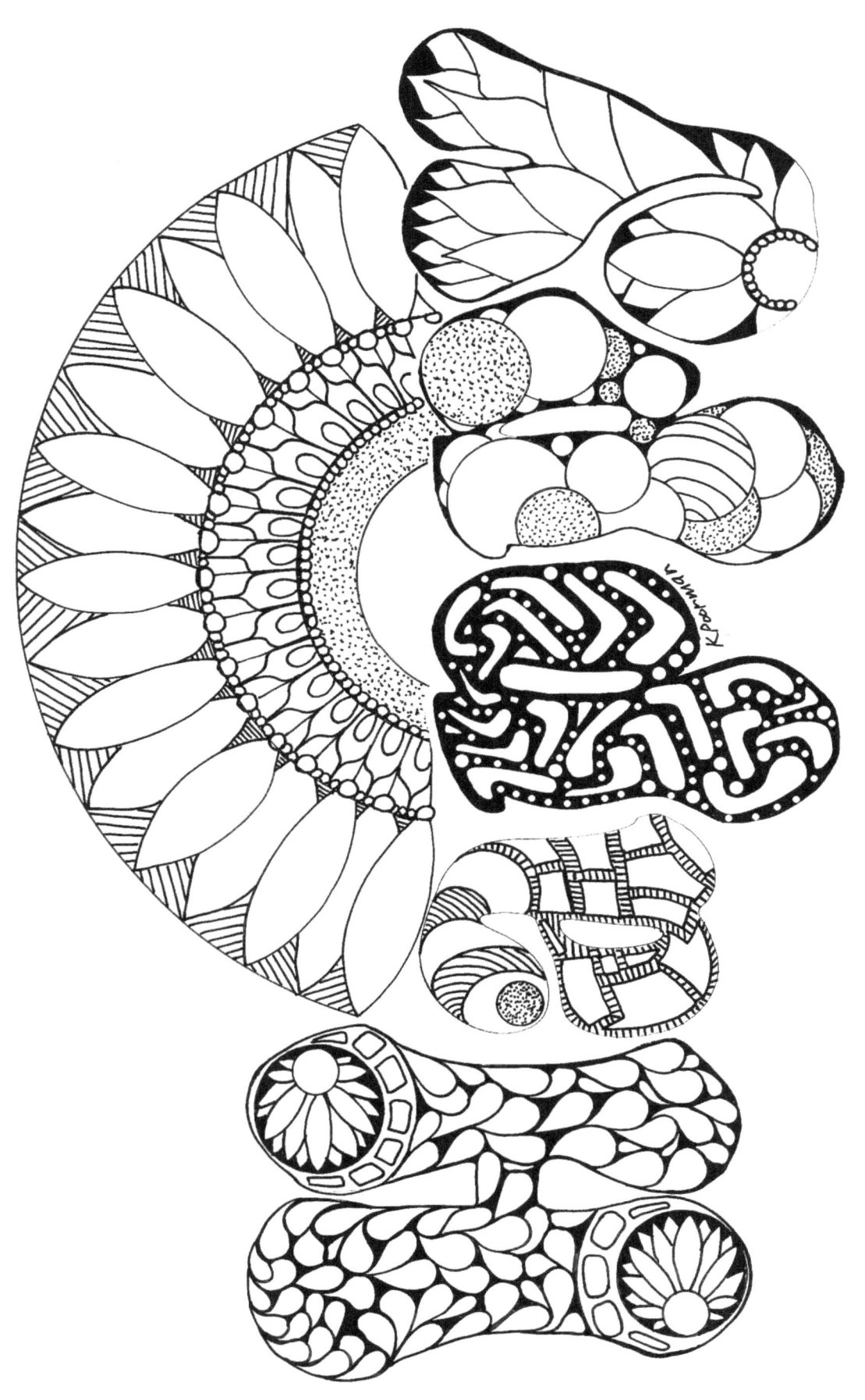

This blank page serves as a blotter page to absorb marker ink that might bleed through while coloring.

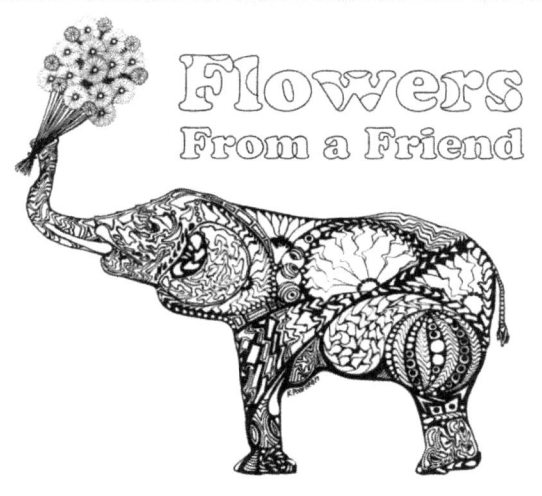

In *Poorman Doodles* book 3.

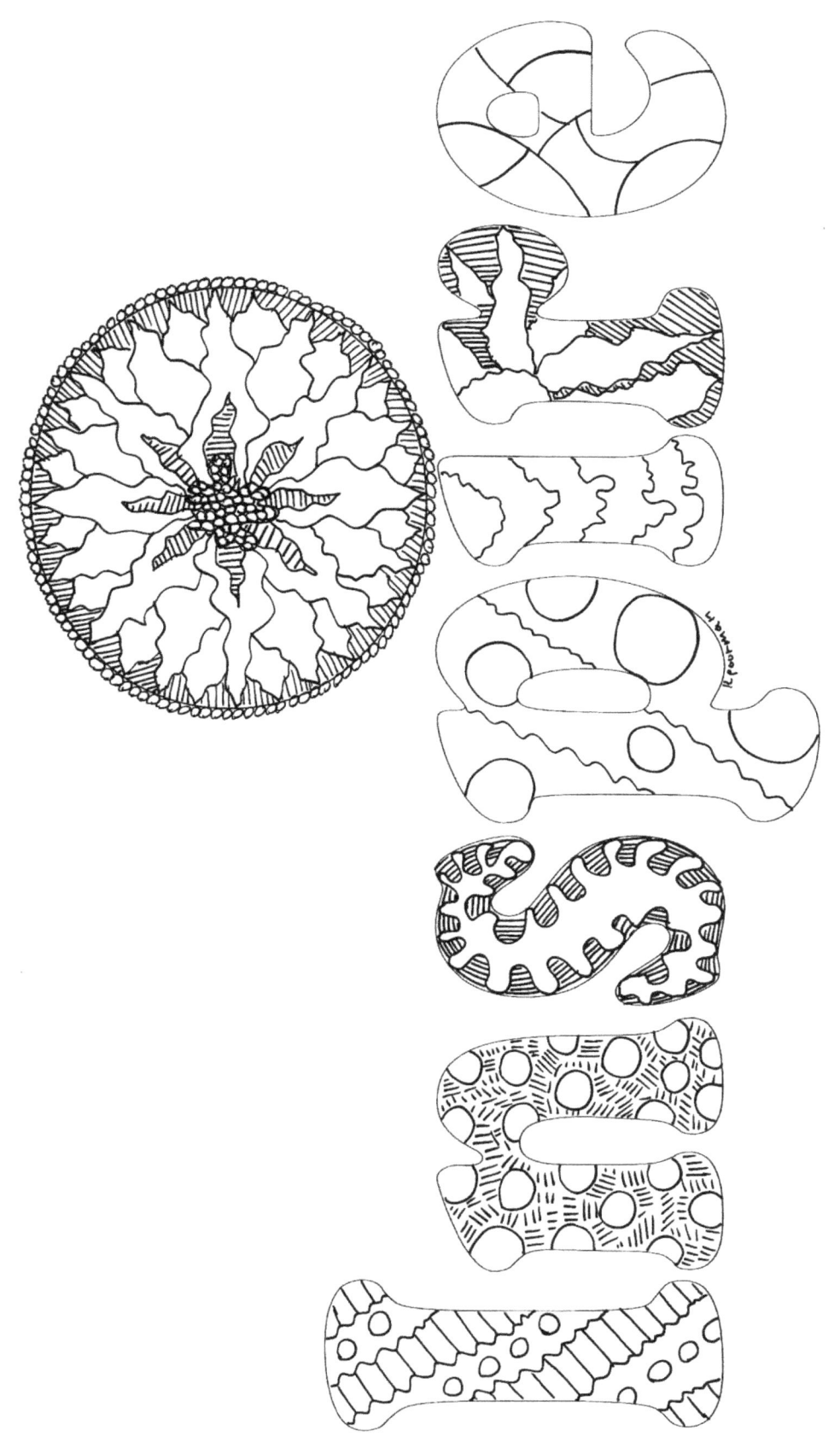

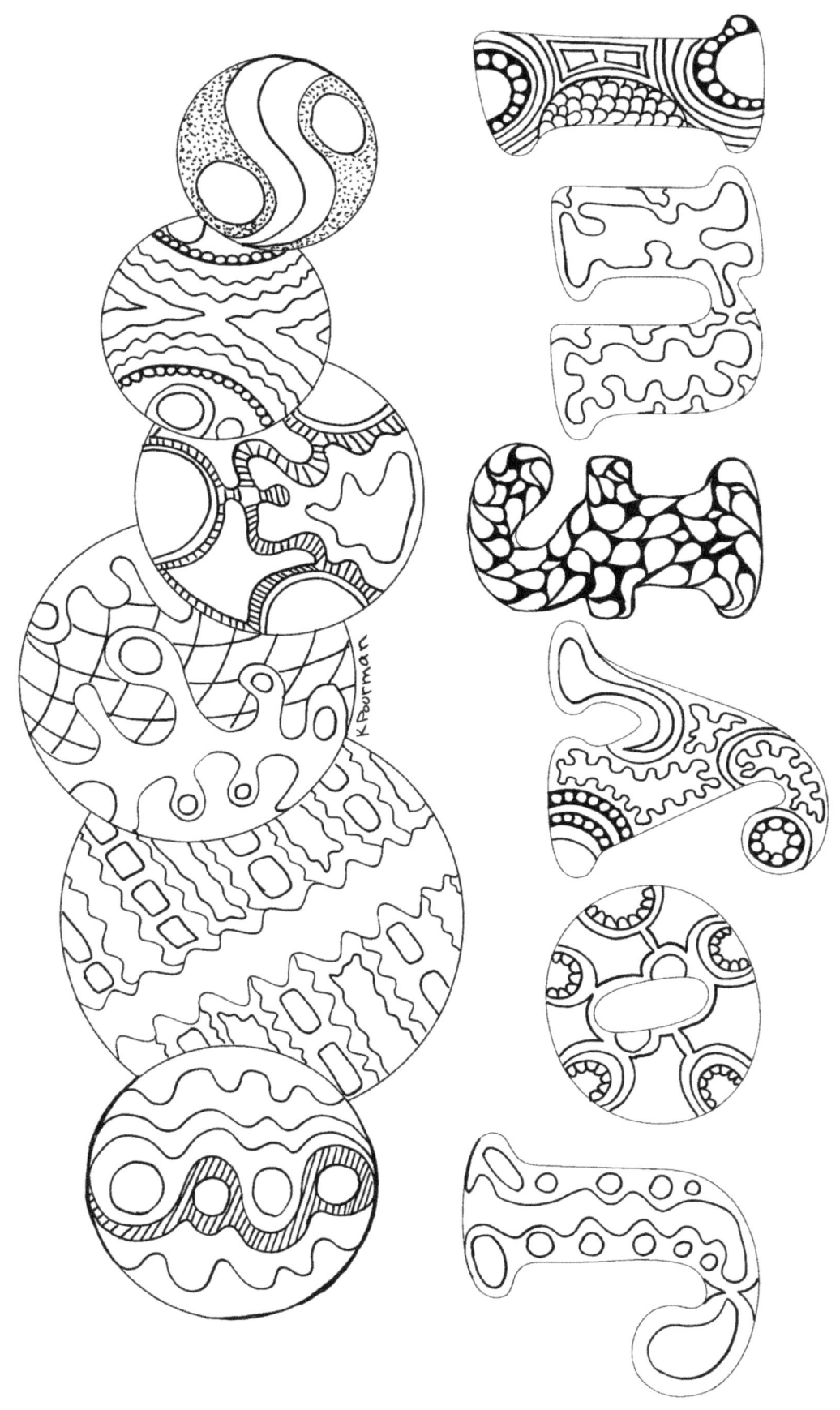

This blank page serves as a blotter page to absorb marker ink that might bleed through while coloring.

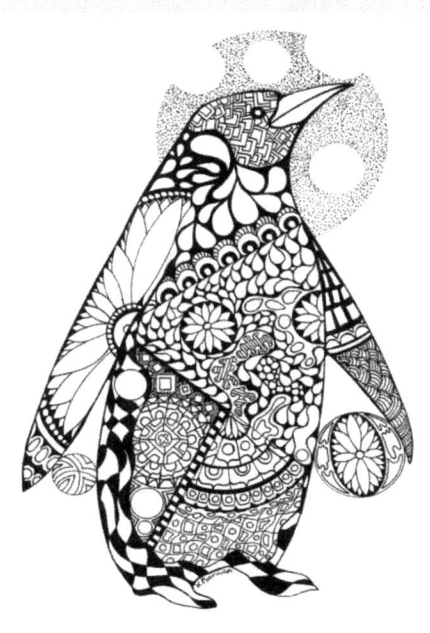

"The Penguin" is in *Poorman Doodles*, Book 5

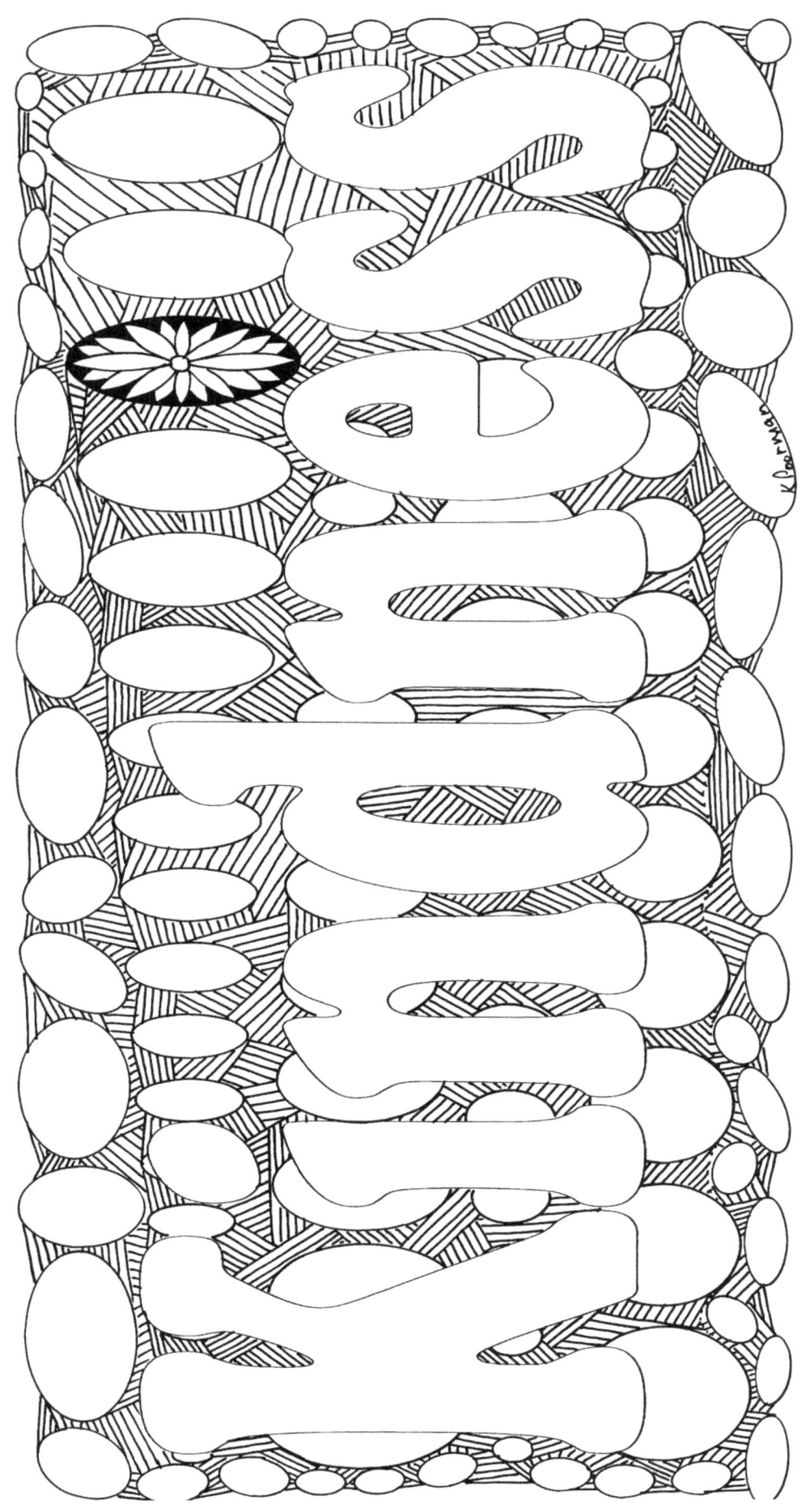

This blank page serves as a blotter page to absorb marker ink that might bleed through while coloring.

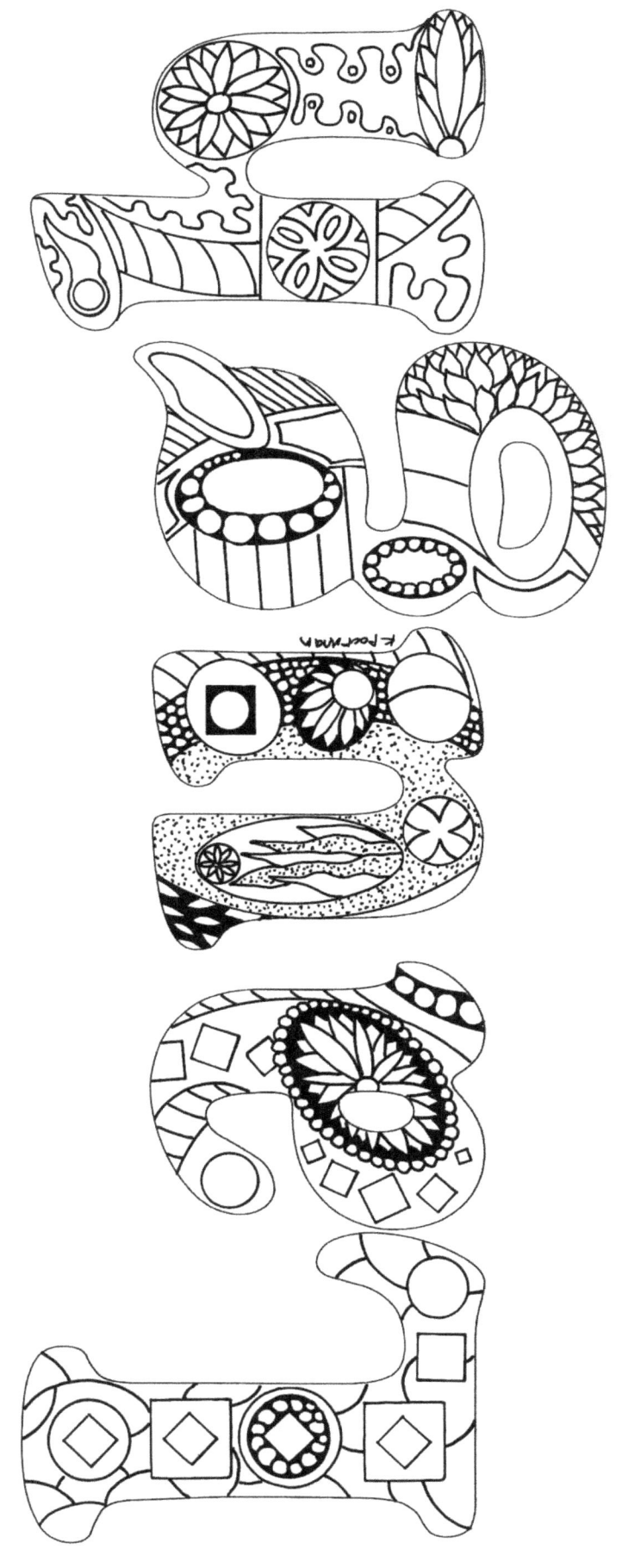

This blank page serves as a blotter page to absorb marker ink that might bleed through while coloring.

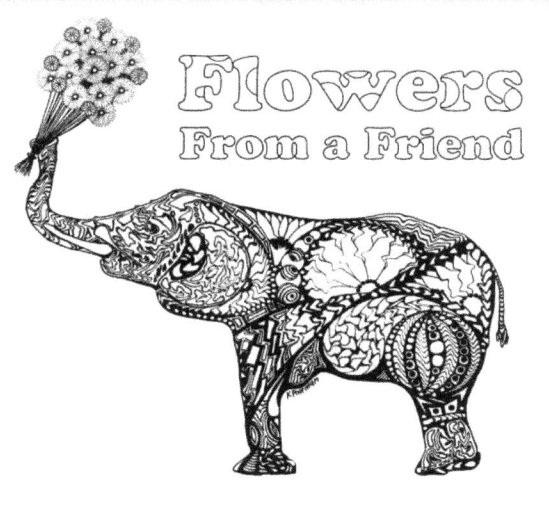

In *Poorman Doodles* book 3.

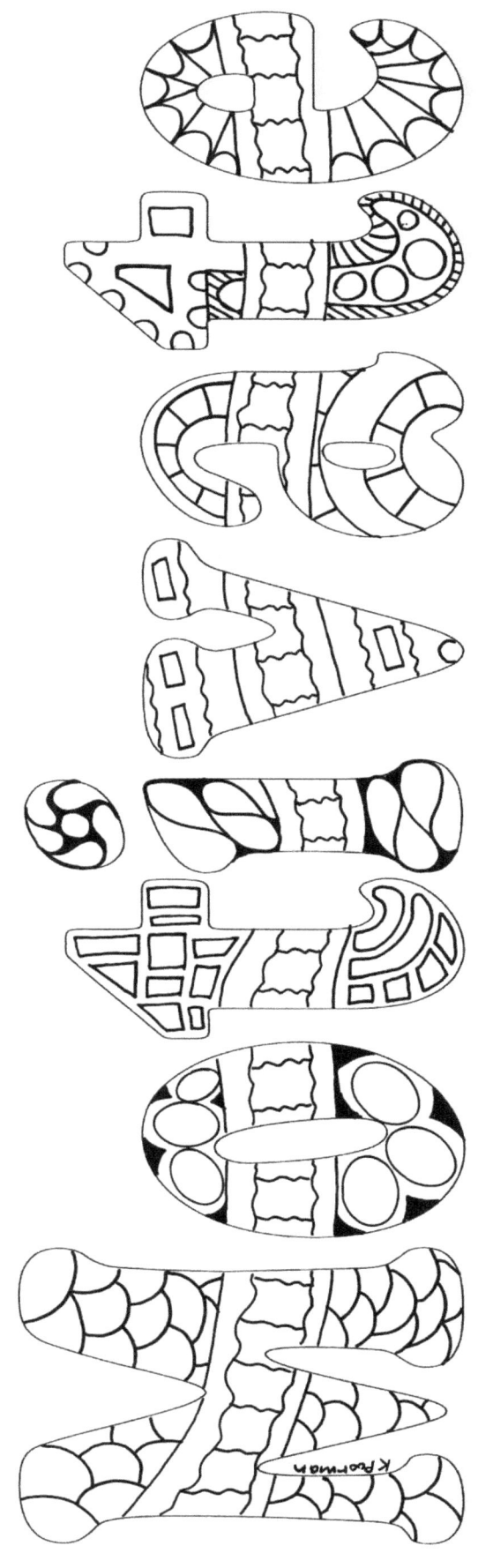

This blank page serves as a blotter
page to absorb marker ink that
might bleed through while coloring.

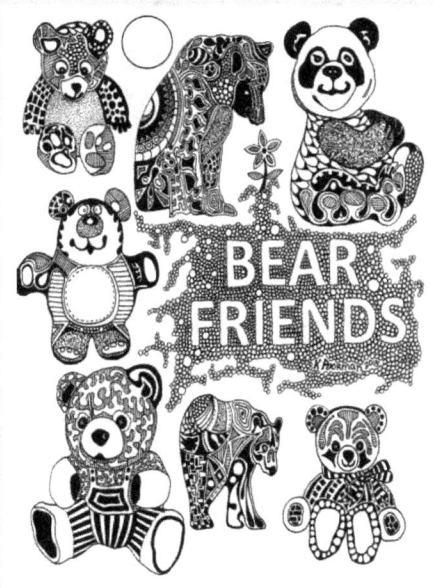

In *Poorman Doodles* book # 1

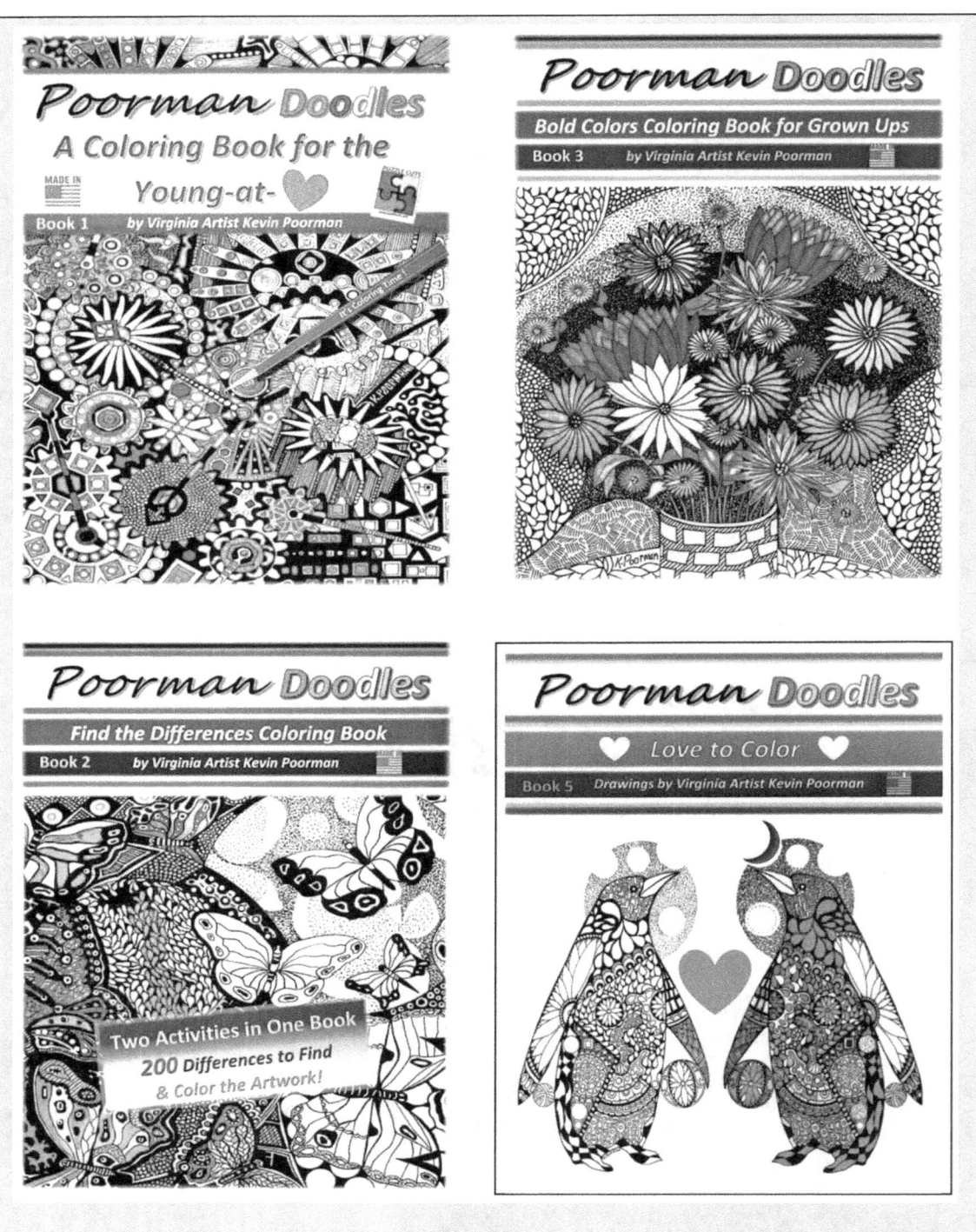

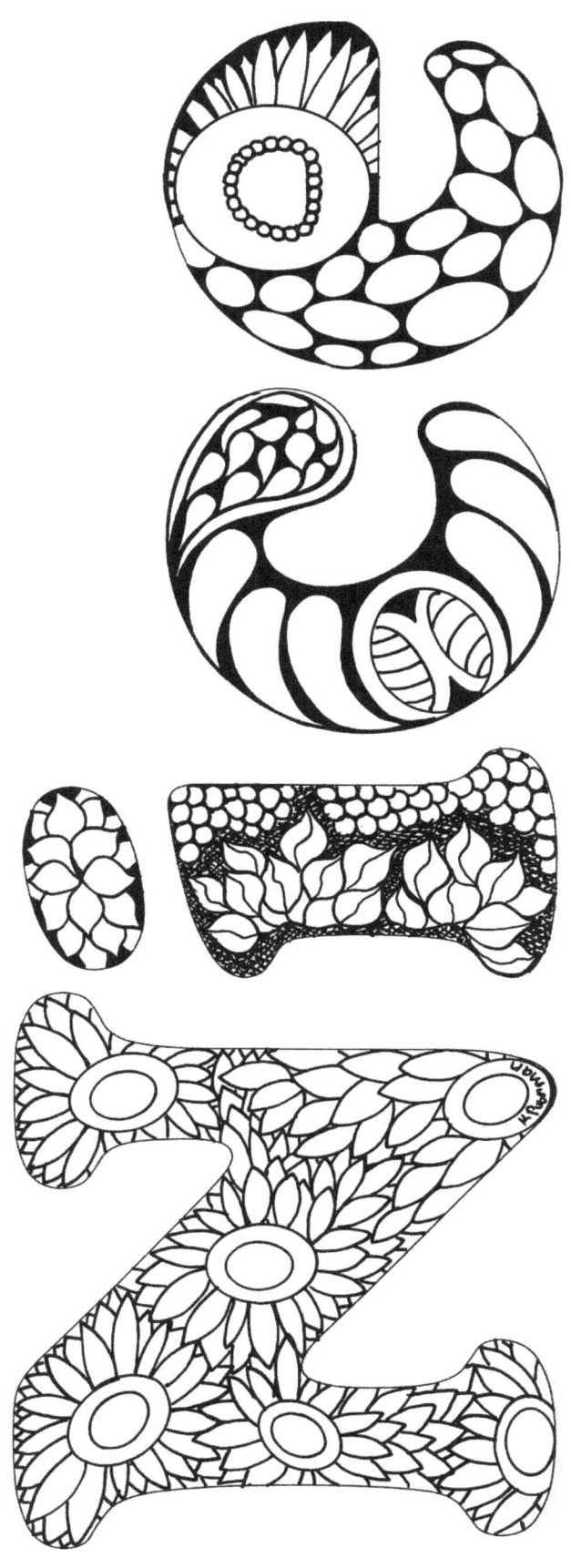

This blank page serves as a blotter page to absorb marker ink that might bleed through while coloring.

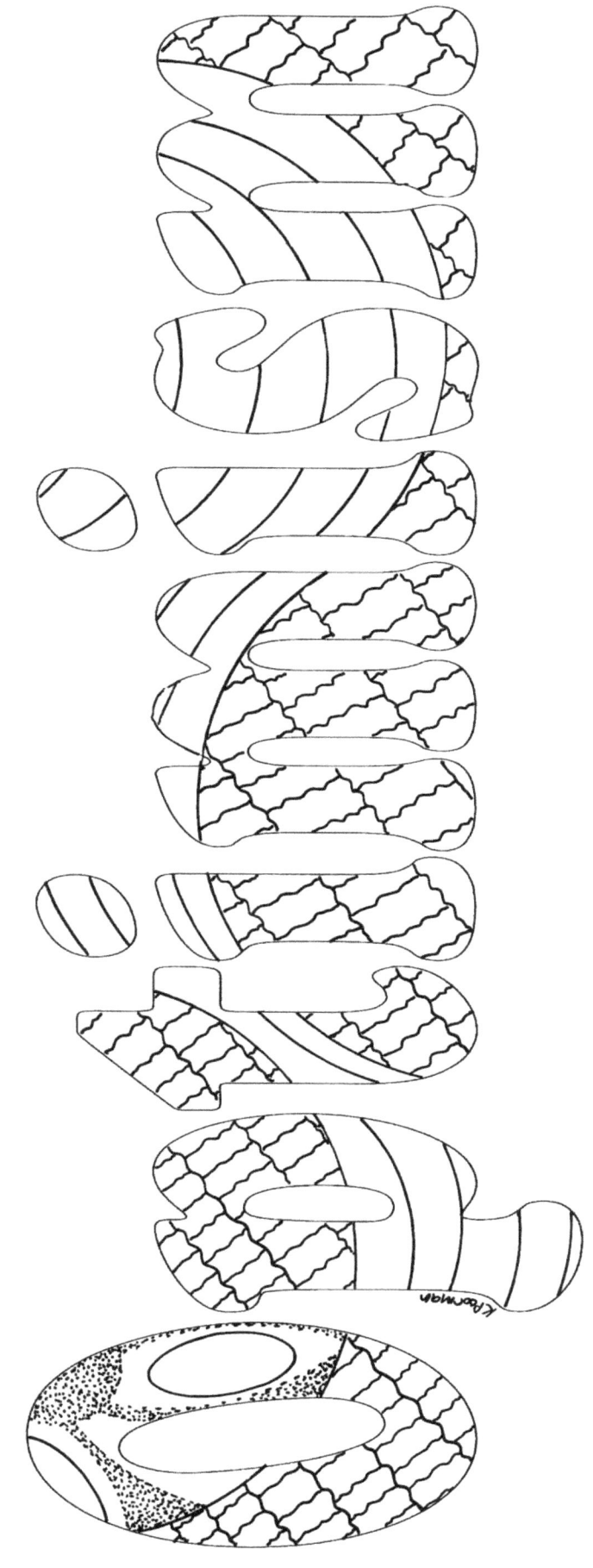

This blank page serves as a blotter page to absorb marker ink that might bleed through while coloring.

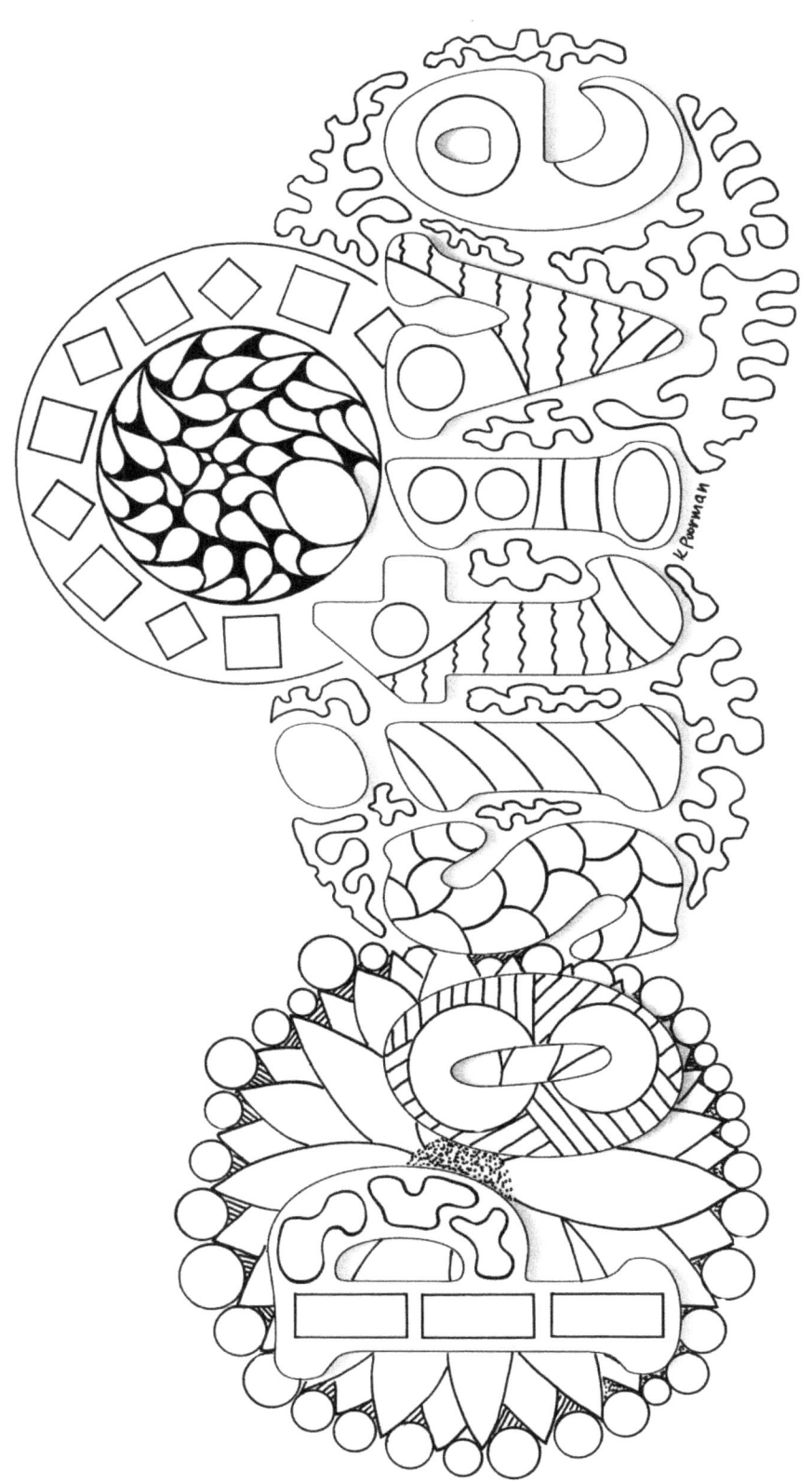

This blank page serves as a blotter page to absorb marker ink that might bleed through while coloring.

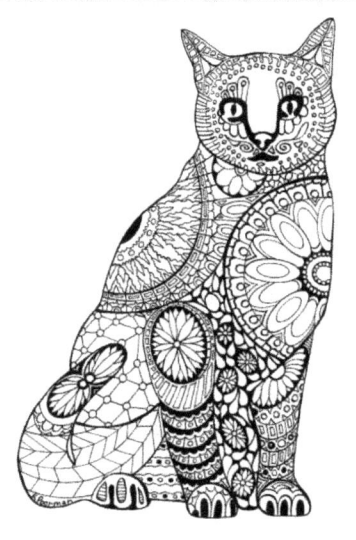

"The Cat" is in *Poorman Doodles*, Book 5

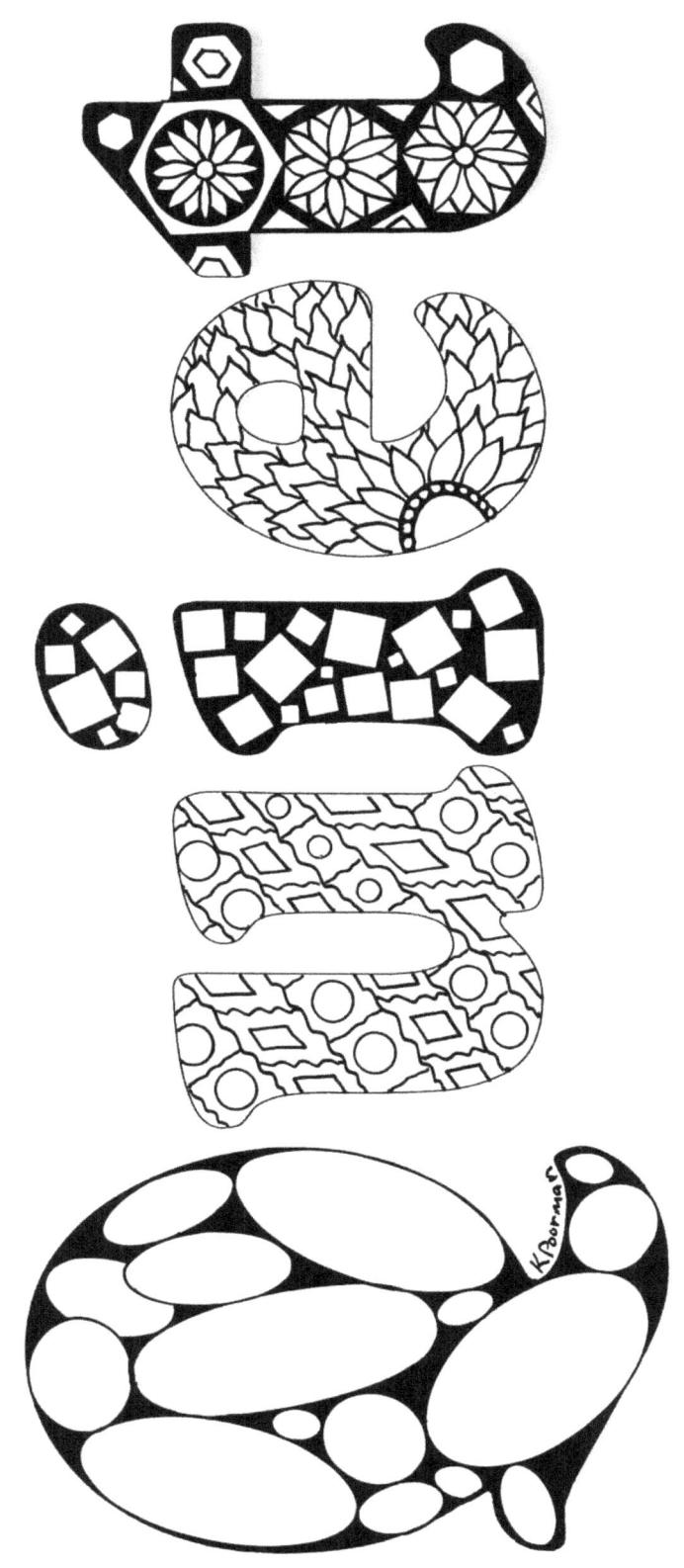

This blank page serves as a blotter
page to absorb marker ink that
might bleed through while coloring.

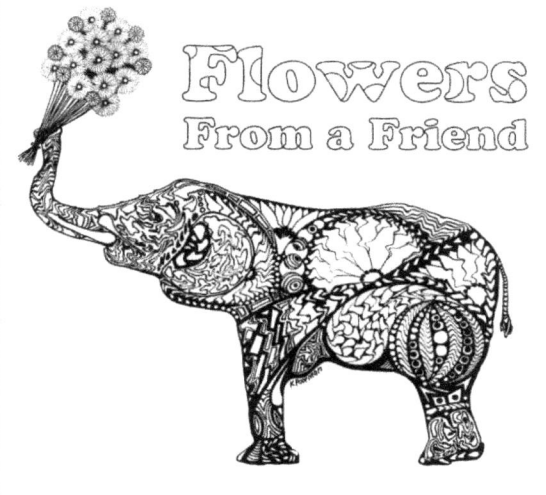

In *Poorman Doodles* book 3.

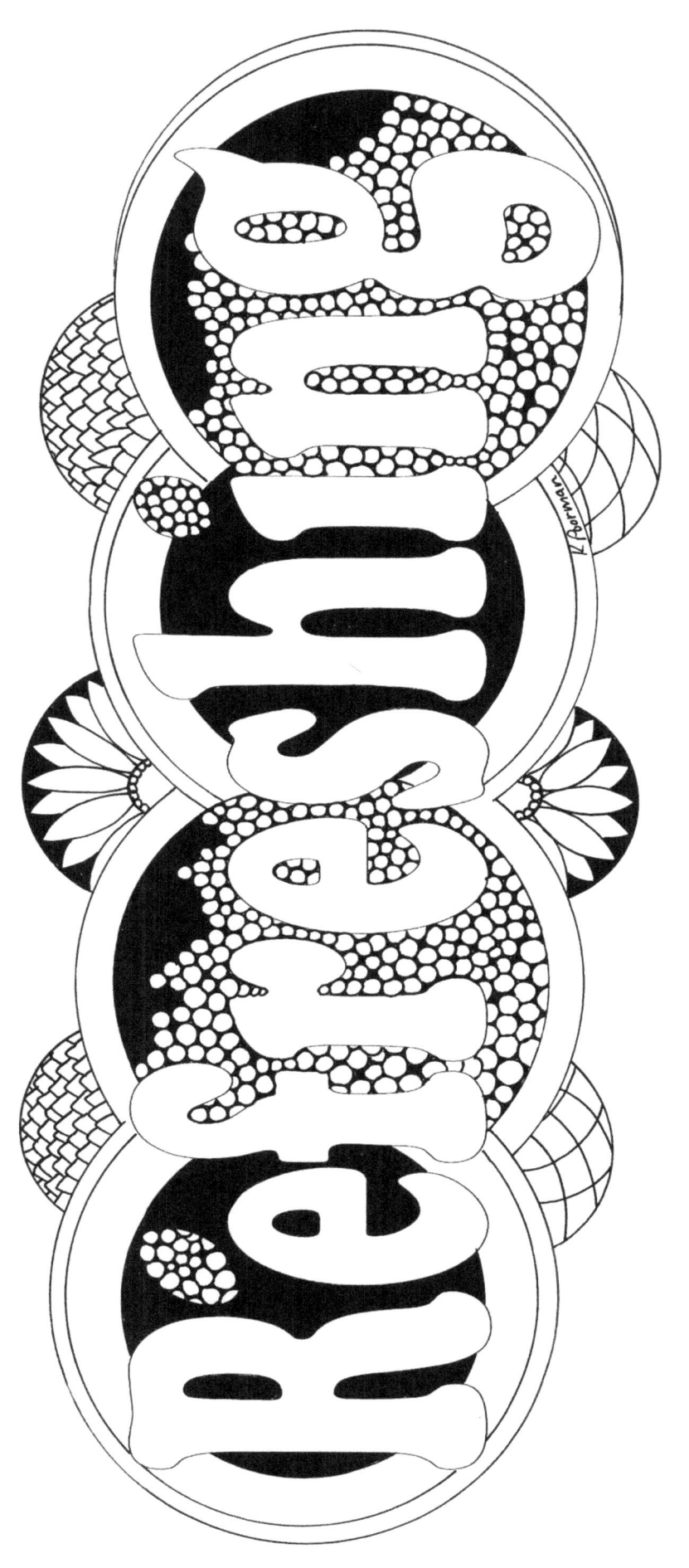

This blank page serves as a blotter page to absorb marker ink that might bleed through while coloring.

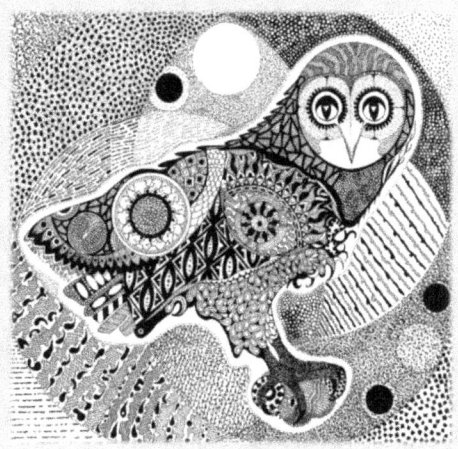

In Poorman Doodles book # 1.

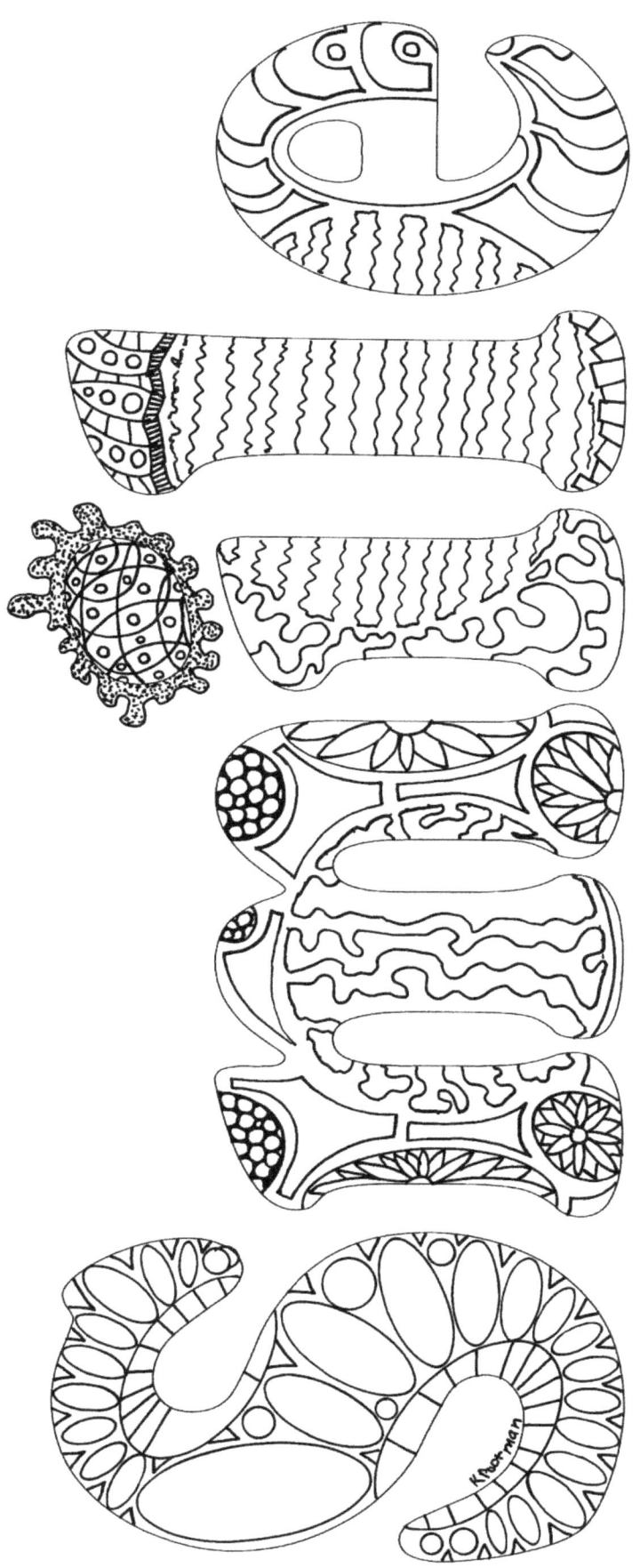

This blank page serves as a blotter
page to absorb marker ink that
might bleed through while coloring.

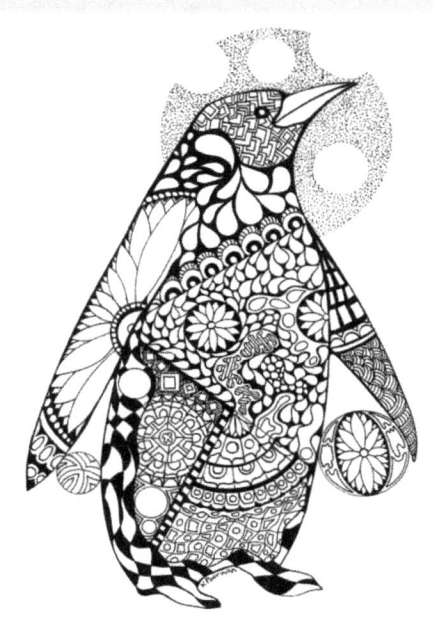

"The Penguin" is in *Poorman Doodles*, Book 5

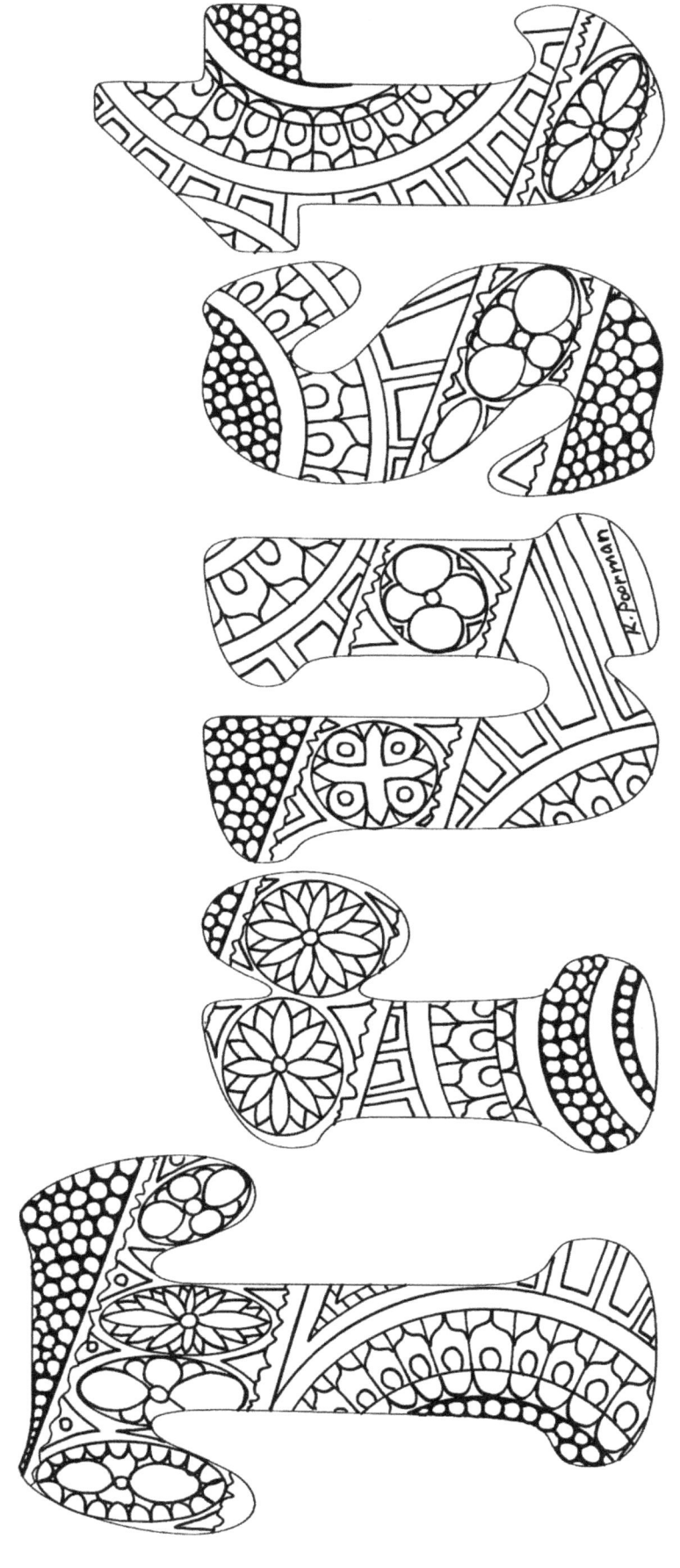

This blank page serves as a blotter page to absorb marker ink that might bleed through while coloring.

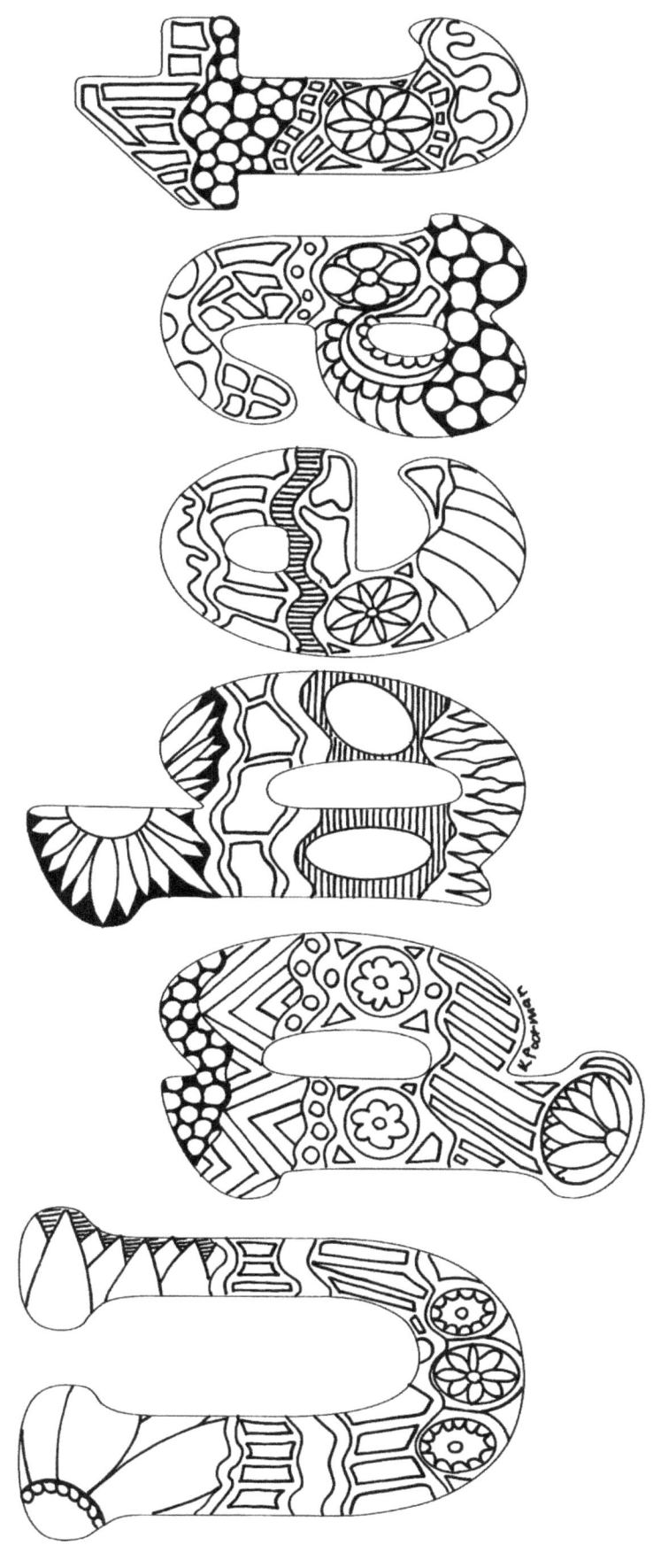

This blank page serves as a blotter
page to absorb marker ink that
might bleed through while coloring.

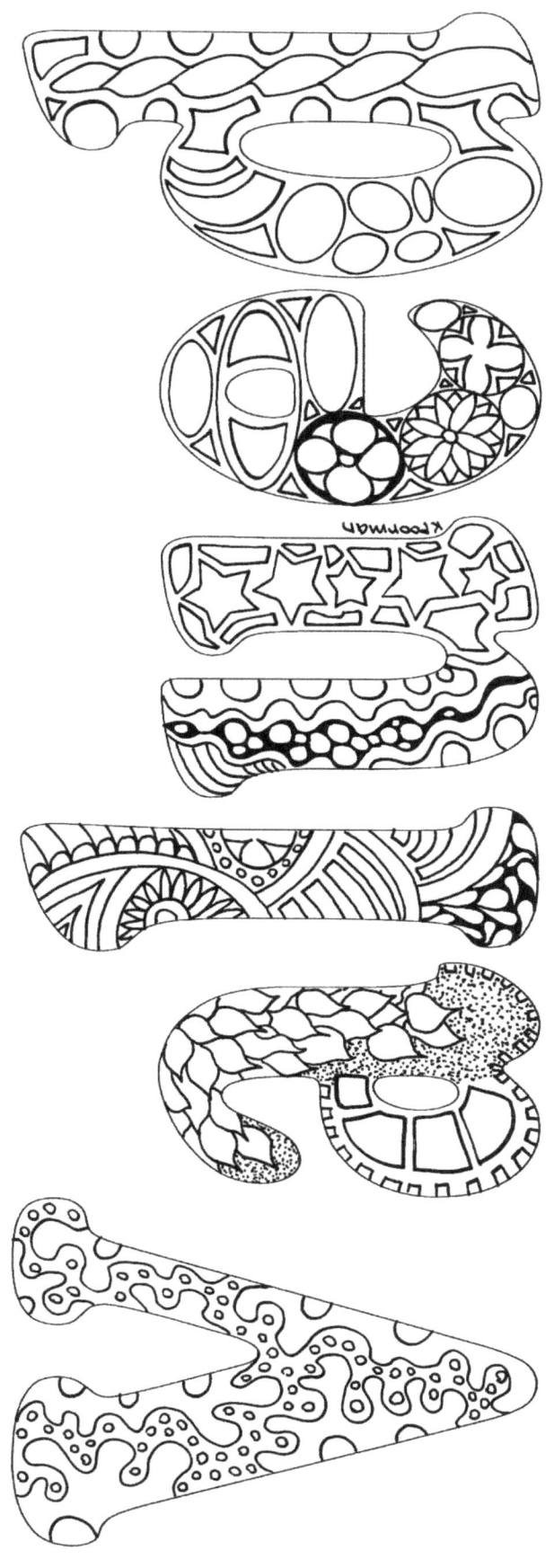

This blank page serves as a blotter
page to absorb marker ink that
might bleed through while coloring.

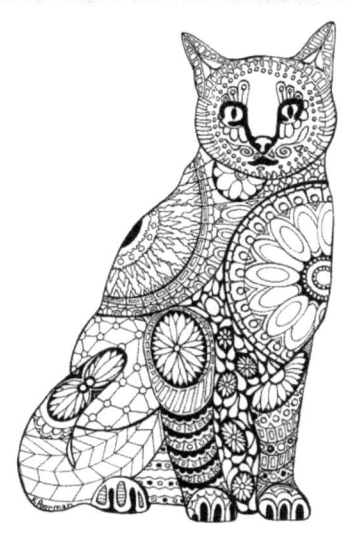

"The Cat" is in *Poorman Doodles*, Book 5

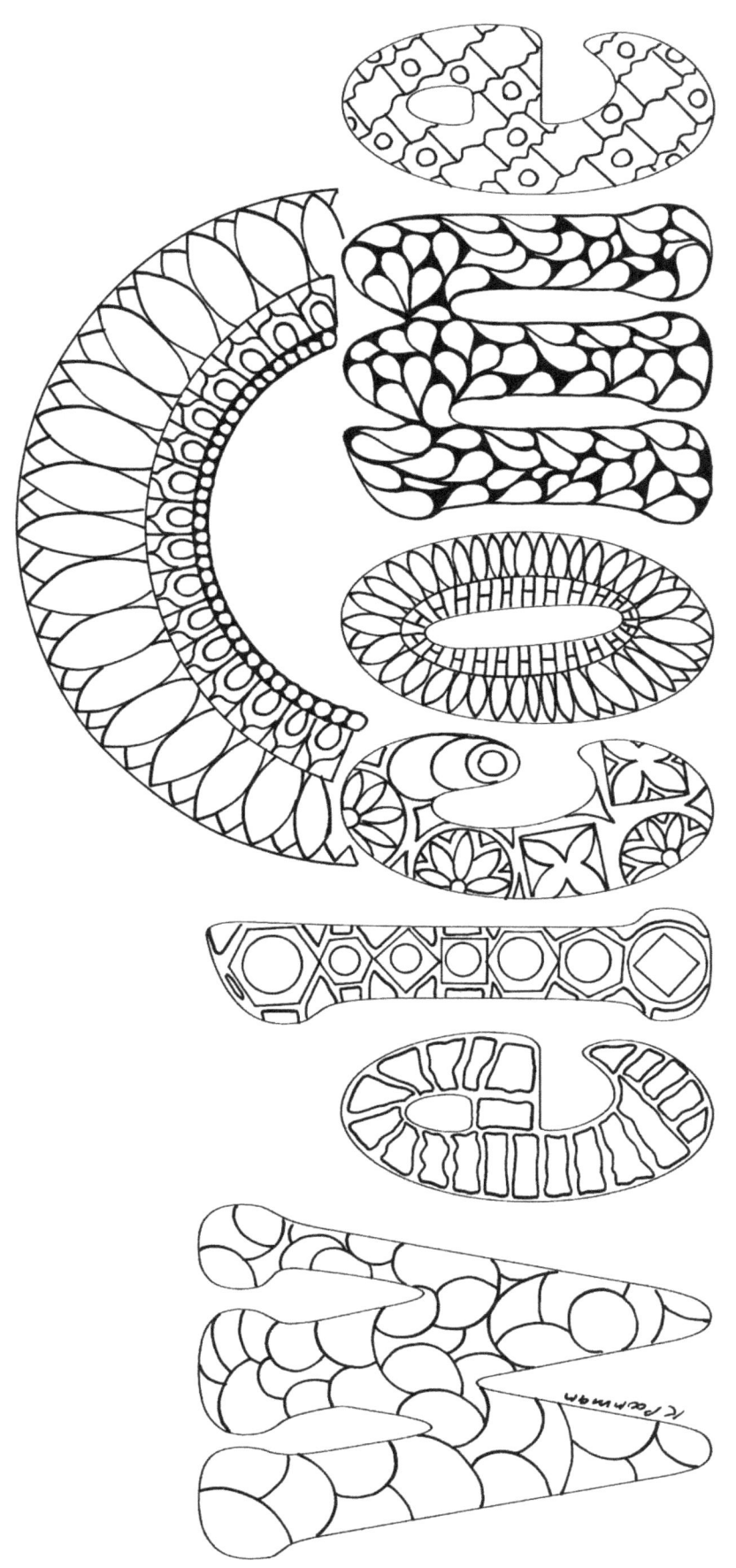

This blank page serves as a blotter page to absorb marker ink that might bleed through while coloring.

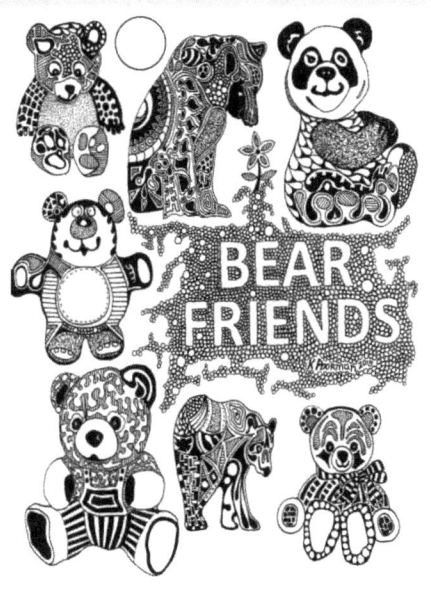

In *Poorman Doodles* book # 1

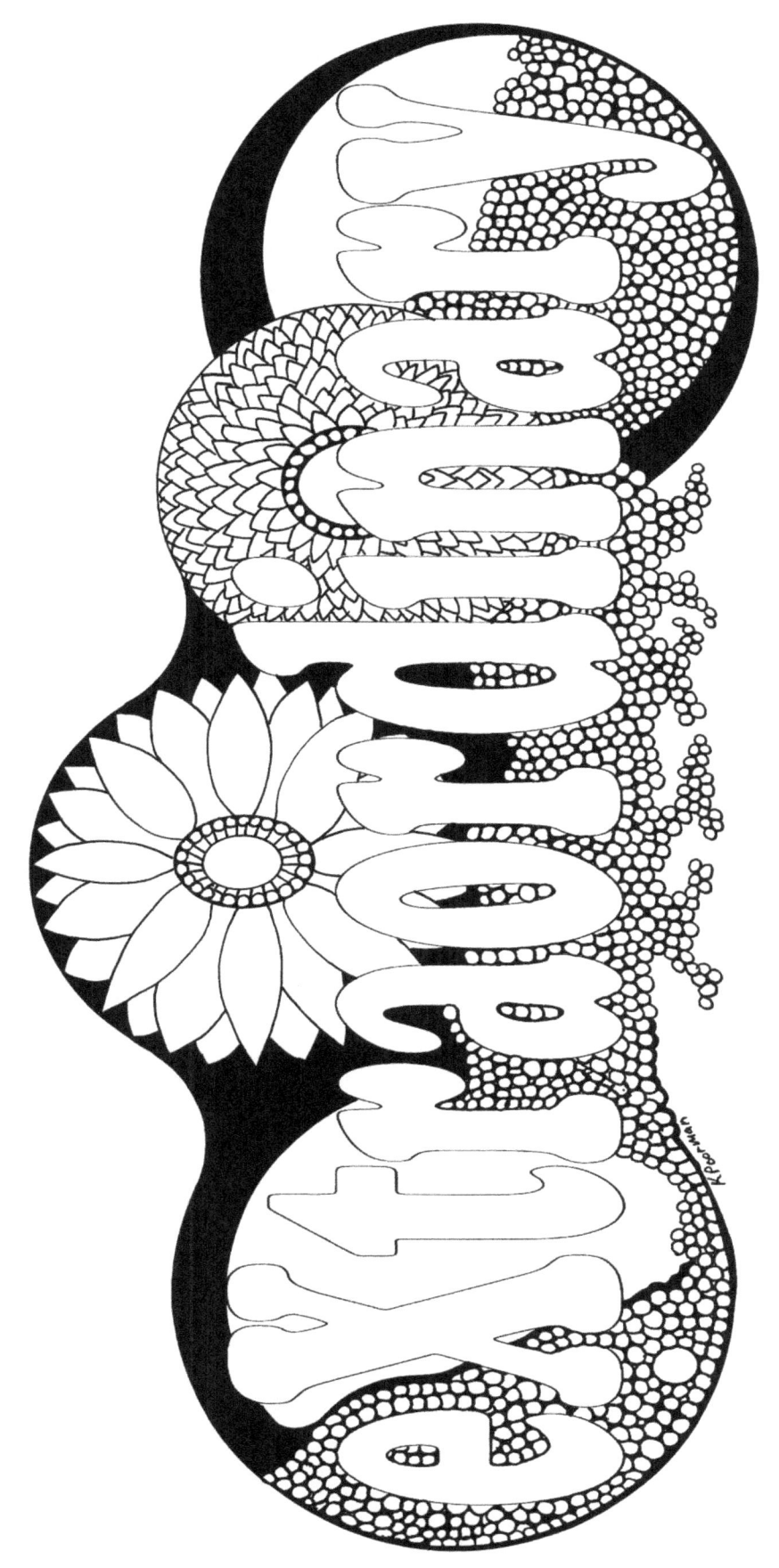

This blank page serves as a blotter page to absorb marker ink that might bleed through while coloring.

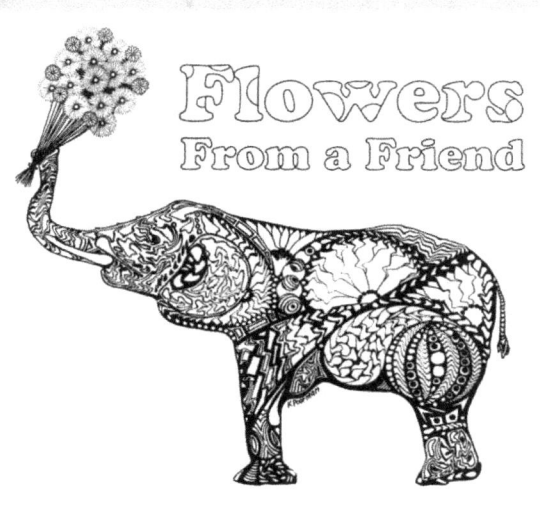

In *Poorman Doodles* book 3.

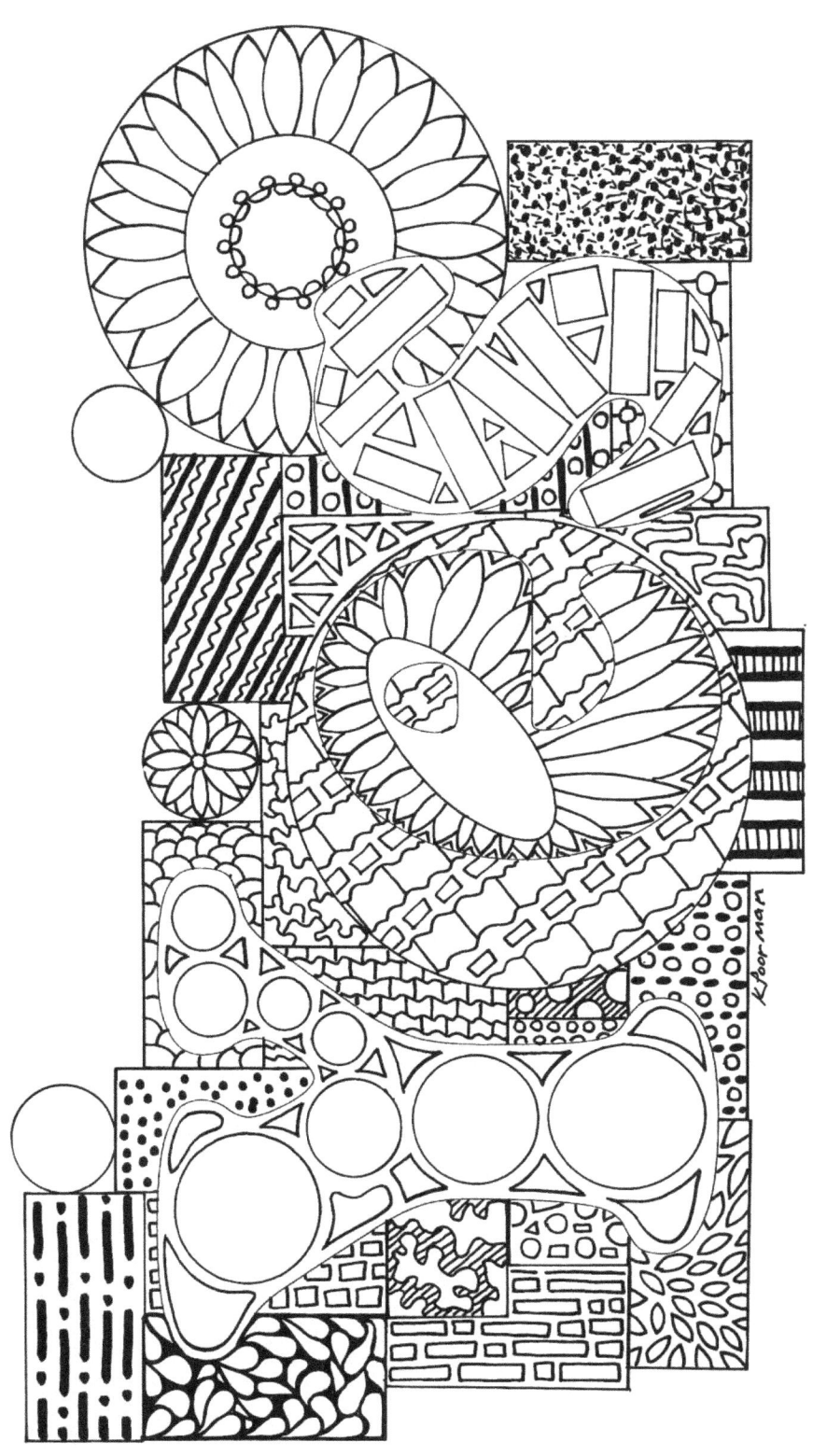

This blank page serves as a blotter page to absorb marker ink that might bleed through while coloring.

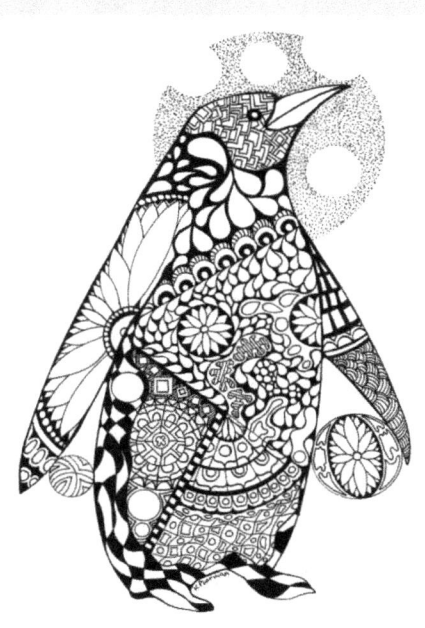

"The Penguin" is in *Poorman Doodles*, Book 5

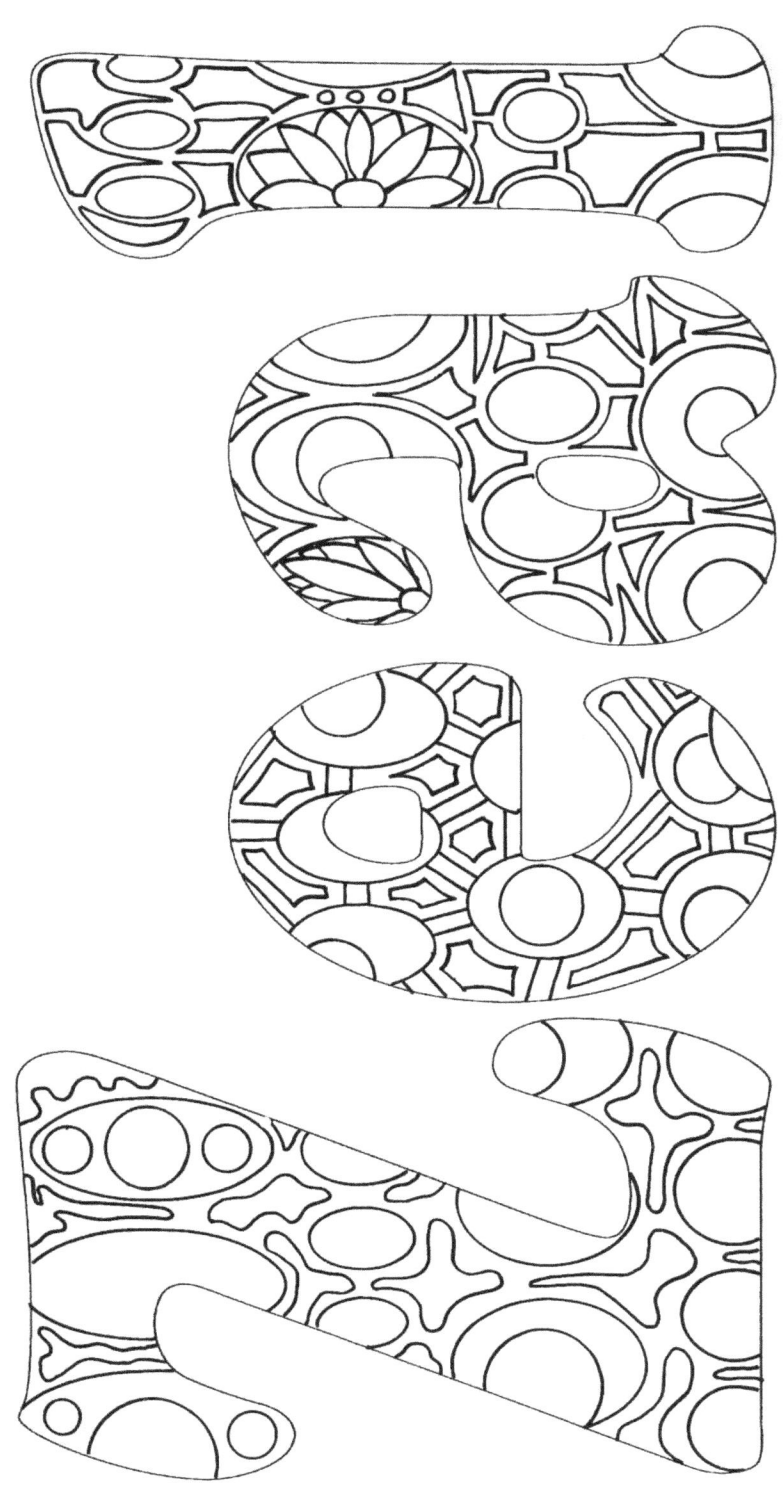

This blank page serves as a blotter page to absorb marker ink that might bleed through while coloring.

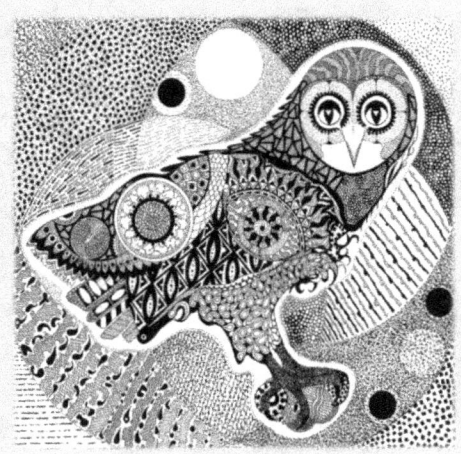

In Poorman Doodles book # 1.

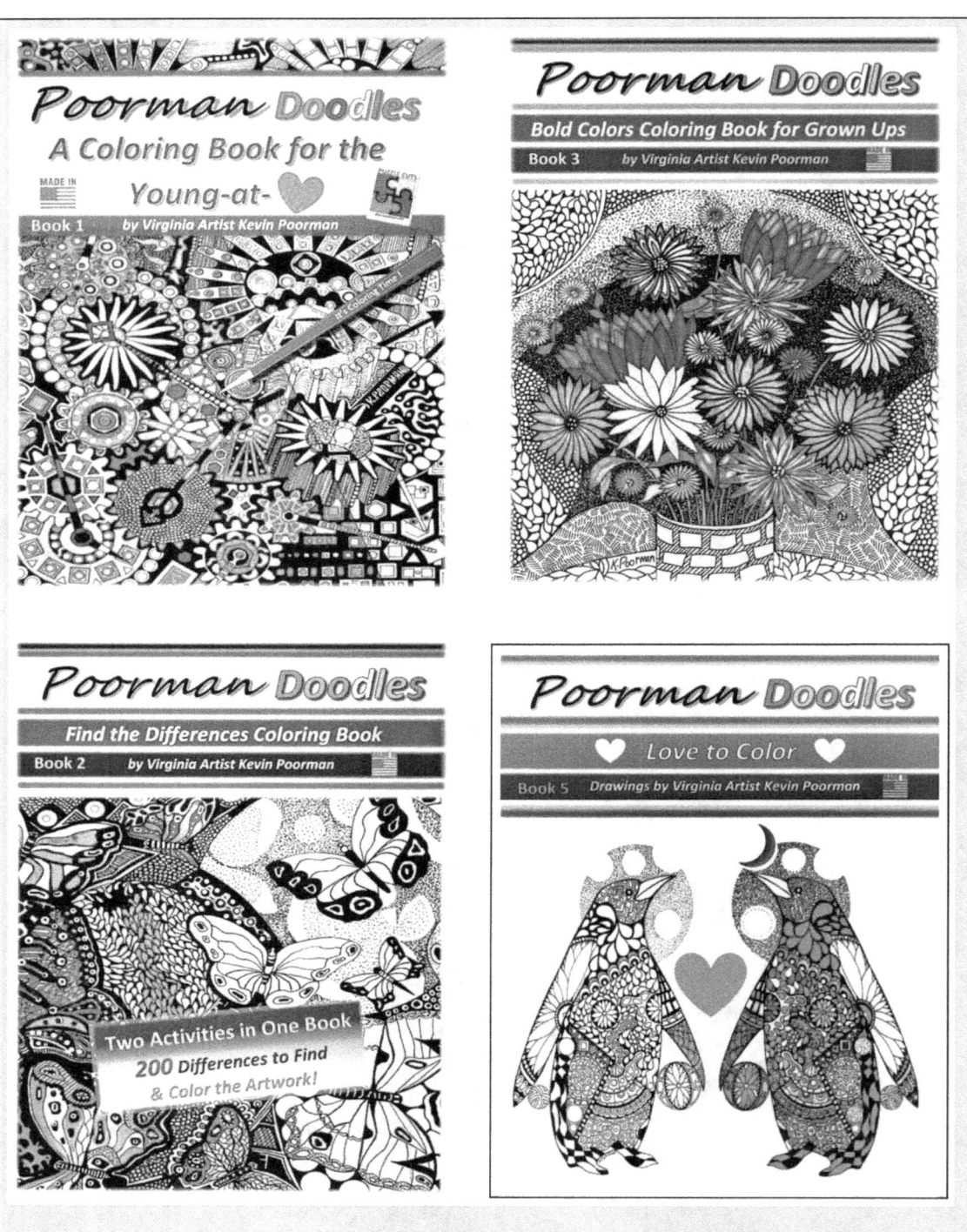